HOW TO ENJOY
Shakespeare

HOW TO ENJOY

Shakespeare

Robert Thomas Fallon

CHICAGO *Ivan R. Dee* 2 0 0 5

HOW TO ENJOY SHAKESPEARE. Copyright © 2005 by Robert Thomas Fallon. All rights reserved, including the right to reproduce this book or portions thereof in any form. For information, address: Ivan R. Dee, Publisher, 1332 North Halsted Street, Chicago 60622. Manufactured in the United States of America and printed on acid-free paper.

Library of Congress Cataloging-in-Publication Data:
Fallon, Robert Thomas.
　How to enjoy Shakespeare / Robert Thomas Fallon.
　　p. cm.
　Includes index
　ISBN 1-56663-618-3 (alk. paper)
　1. Shakespeare, William, 1564–1616—Technique. 2. Shakespeare, William, 1564–1616—Appreciation. 3. Shakespeare, William, 1564–1616—Dramatic production. 4. Theater audiences. I. Title.

PR2995.F35 2005
822.3'3—dc22
　　　　　　　　　　　　　　　　　　　2004053689

For Whitney and Laurel,
that they may enjoy

Contents

Prologue

SHAKESPEARE'S WORLD is in many ways not our own, and the strangeness of its time and language can impose impediments to both understanding and pleasure. My purpose is to sweep away some of that surface strangeness, enabling a playgoer to savor the riches that lie beneath. Shakespeare's characters, though they may be kings and queens, can be as familiar to us as our fathers and mothers. His locales, Italy and the ancient world, Bohemia and Illyria, could just as well be our village or city block. And his plots, though they deal in medieval war, court intrigue, and occult powers, could be episodes in the passage of any single life. The language admittedly takes some getting used to, but the glory of these plays is well worth our patience and perseverance.

Instances of this pattern of familiarity abound in plays that can be seen during any theater season—*King Lear, Hamlet, Romeo and Juliet*—but they are equally abundant in some of the lesser known and infrequently produced works—*Titus Andronicus, Timon of Athens, Pericles.* I shall draw on some of the latter from time to time, in order to illustrate the rich variety of Shakespeare's imaginative reach, the dazzling scope of his achievement. These occasional allusions may have the added benefit of encouraging a theatergoer to attend a performance of one of these generally ignored plays when the rare opportunity is offered.

These pages are divided into five short sections, each dealing with an aspect of Shakespeare that may seem troublesome to the playgoer who comes upon his works unprepared:

- The language, which can be daunting.
- The themes, or ideas, that lie embedded in the lines, reflecting the timeless truths of human nature.
- The staging of the plays, that is, the setting of the action and the theater for which Shakespeare wrote.
- The variety of characters.
- The plots, which can be convoluted.

We shall of necessity revisit some characters, episodes, and even individual lines in separate sections. Hamlet is a character, to begin with, but his action or inaction represents a theme as well, and his lines illustrate the richness of Shakespeare's language. The same may be said of Prince Hal, Othello, and King Lear, so they will reappear from time to time in different contexts. A timely glance at one, or all, of these sections will, it is hoped, enhance a theatergoer's pleasure and understanding in watching a performance.

These matters, and others, are examined in greater depth and detail in my *A Theatergoer's Guide to Shakespeare*, which surveys the plots, in *A Theatergoer's Guide to Shakespeare's Themes*, and in *A Theatergoer's Guide to Shakespeare's Characters*, all published by Ivan R. Dee of Chicago.

Prologue

I am indebted to Ivan Dee, whose idea this was, and to Dr. James A. Butler for his kindly counsel, encouragement, and friendship. And I am grateful, once more, to the members of The Shakspere (sic) Society of Philadelphia for their insights.

HOW TO ENJOY
Shakespeare

I

Language

ANYONE WHO COMES unprepared to Shakespeare's plays in performance will be disconcerted by the fact that the characters do not talk to one another in the familiar patterns of everyday speech. Those new to Shakespeare may well ask how it is possible to enjoy a play when they can't understand half the words being said. They may wonder at the rapt attention of their fellow playgoers, whose eyes are riveted on the stage and can be seen to smile, laugh, or weep at times, then burst into wild applause as the curtain falls. Beginners may well begin to suspect that they may have missed something important along the way.

This initial strangeness arises in part from the fact that the actors and actresses are for the most part speaking in verse, which has rules of its own. A playwright hopes to move an audience, and poetry is the language of emotion. In its rhythms, its rhymes, and its images, it recaptures moments of joy and despair, of fear and longing, that are common to the human experience—the stuff of life. Poetry, in this regard, shares many qualities with music: what words are to a sonnet, notes are to a sonata. Both strive for similar effects: to evoke thought and move emotion. Words may be more effective in sparking thought and notes in arousing emotion, but both draw on the bond between mind and body. Music, because it is the more familiar medium of the two, can help us understand the appeal of poetry.

There can be little doubt of the power of music to arouse the passions. It can send the spirit soaring, recall the sorrow of lost love, or incite anger at injustice. It can set the toe tapping and the feet marching; it can send a chill down the spine, bring a tear to the eye, and propel the body into a wild dance. Poetry, like music, touches a deep core of human sentiment lying beneath the level of the conscious mind, something elemental to our nature. The most memorable of Shakespeare's passages are both moving and profound precisely because their poetry shares with music two of its essential qualities, its rhythm and its sound.

RHYTHM

The rhythm of music resonates on the basic pulses of life—the beating of the heart, the pumping of blood through the veins, the intake and release of breath, the measured pace of walking. These are functions that the primitive brain controls, actions that the conscious mind takes little notice of. The beat of music slips past waking thought and appeals directly to these unconscious rhythms of life, throbbing along the thin matrix of nerves that twitch the muscles and excite the blood. Drums have traditionally roused men to battle, there with them in primitive war dances and the measured tread of more modern armies marching to the sound of cannon. If you doubt the power of rhythm, observe the frenzied response of a rock concert audience as the singers shout out some mindless phrase over and over at the close of a number while the band blares the same notes in a rising crescendo of pure, naked BEAT.

In other regards, there is something about rhythm that puts the human spirit in touch with all the reiterate tempos of nature—the rise and setting of the sun, the passage of seasons, the bloom and fading of a flower, the yearly migration of birds, the waves that rise and recede on moonlit shores. The recurrent cadence of music reminds us that we are participants in a vast pattern of events, not as the separate beings our conscious mind would have us, but as one of many, as indistinguishable from all others as the grains of sand upon a beach. That rhythm, then, tells us we are part of a sublime whole, a grand and mysterious entity that pulses through the stem of a rose and circles the stars.

In another respect, music alternates between constancy and change. The repetition of a sequence of notes satisfies expectation; at the same time variations on these same sounds capture the attention and delight the ear. The entire first movement of Beethoven's Fifth Symphony is a series of variations on its first four dramatic chords. Folk music can have endless verses, telling a tale of love or loss, alternating with the repetition of the same chorus. Constancy and change, repetition and variety—life swings between them. The routine of a workaday existence is relieved by an occasional holiday; it is enlivened by a new love or a birth, and is unsettled by a death. Constancy comforts the spirit, change animates it. We are not content without the one and cannot be said to live fully without the other. In the same way, music repeats a theme with variations that discover different shades of meaning in the notes. In its repetition and variety, then, it echoes the essential patterns of life.

The lines of Shakespeare's poetry are alive with alternating rhythms, though as with music we are often unaware of their effect upon us. Some knowledge of his meters, however, can enhance our enjoyment of a play's musical qualities.

For the most part, any single line in Shakespeare consists of ten syllables, or five "feet" of two syllables each. It is a measure that students of poetry call "pentameter." Shakespeare does vary the pattern at times, reducing the feet to four in songs or incantations: "Dóuble, dóuble, tóil and tróuble" (I add stresses here initially to illustrate the meter). The variety is achieved, again for the most part, by stressing one or the other, or both, of the syllables in each foot, providing patterns to which those same students of poetry have given names. In the "iambic" foot, the stress is on the second syllable, as in "abóut" or "enóugh." In the "trochaic" it is on the first, as in "óver" and "únder." And in the "spondaic" it is on both, as in "Dón't shóot" or "Kéep quíet." There are others, including one in which neither syllable is stressed, but these three—the iambic, the trochaic, and the spondaic—are the dominant meters of Shakespeare's poetry.

Although these distinctions may seem overly academic— with Greek names, no less—they represent in fact the familiar rhythms of everyday speech and writing, particularly those intended to appeal to the emotions, which, as has been noted, is the particular end of poetic expression. The iambic is found in inspirational oratory—for example in Abraham Lincoln's "a ná|tion óf | the péople, bý | the péo|ple, fór | the péo|ple," or Martin Luther King's, "I háve | a dréam." The trochaic is equally familiar, to be found in an impatient parent's admonition, "Gó and | cléan your | róom" or "Eát your | cárrots." The spondaic meter is employed for emphasis and impact, such as the shouting of political slogans, "Dówn wíth Jónes!" or "Úp wíth Smíth!"; the challenge hurled across the barricades of protest during the 1960s, "Héll nó, │ wé wón't │ gó!"; or the chant of aroused football fans, "Wé wíll, │ wé wíll, │ róck yóu!"

These are the rhythms, then, that we often express in our more intense moments. And it is the meters of poetry that capture the intensity of those moments. Some of Shakespeare's most familiar lines reflect the iambic meter (you're on your own now): "Farewell, Othello's occupation's gone!" and Romeo's "What light through yonder window breaks? It is the east / And Juliet is the sun." We recall as well King Lear's lament, "I am more sinned against than sinning." The trochaic simply reverses the stress to achieve the same effect, usually in the first foot of a line, as in Othello's, "Villain, be sure you prove my love a whore," "Impudent strumpet," and "Soft you, a word or two before you go." The two meters, as mentioned, reflect the predominant rhythms of the spoken word. It is interesting to note how many of Shakespeare's prose passages reflect their use as well, as in Prince Hal's iambic insults of Falstaff: "thou claybrained guts, thou knotty-pated fool, thou whoreson, obscene, greasy tallow-catch." We may not know what a "tallow-catch" is, but we can relish the delicious rhythm.

Shakespeare at times employs the spondaic for a highly dramatic effect, often in a line of repeated words, as in Lear's "Then kill, kill, kill, kill, kill, kill!" "No, no, no, no! Let's away to prison." and "Howl! Howl! Howl! O, you are men of stones." The poet can soften the effect of such repetitions by varying the meter, as in the trochaic measure of Lear's lament for Cordelia, "Thou'lt come no more, / Never, never, never,

never, never." As a poetic device, however, the spondaic foot can be overdone, and Shakespeare mocks its excessive use in Bottom's comic death as Pyramus in *A Midsummer Night's Dream*: "Now, die, die, die, die, die." As with the trochaic meter, Shakespeare will combine the spondaic with others in a single line to achieve emphasis, as in Lear's "Blow, winds, and crack your cheeks! Rage! Blow!" and "Strike flat the thick rotundity o'th'world!"

To achieve poetic variety—constancy and change—Shakespeare will on occasion include all three meters in a single line. As Othello approaches the sleeping Desdemona, he intones a solemn chant: "It is the cause, it is the cause, my soul. / Let me not name it to you, you chaste stars!" In the second line, "Let me" is trochaic, the middle feet roughly iambic, and the final "chaste stars!" spondaic.

The need to sustain both the meter and the pentameter line caused Shakespeare at times to take liberties with words: he combined them, omitted them, inverted their normal order, called for them to be pronounced in unfamiliar ways, and punctuated them curiously. This practice accounts in part for the difficulty modern readers and audiences may have with his language. Knowing his devices can help dispel some of our perplexity about what is being said.

In the matter of punctuation, for example, remember that Shakespeare wrote his plays to be performed on stage, not read in books. His commas, periods, and apostrophes informed actors how he wanted his lines spoken. Indeed, he followed a long tradition in this practice. Punctuation was first introduced into written language by ancient Greek playwrights to indicate where actors should pause in delivering a line. Shakespeare drew attention to the practice by deliberately misplacing punctuation in Peter Quince's muddled prologue to *Pyramus and Thisbe* in *A Midsummer Night's Dream*, resulting in such comic distortions as:

> We do not come, as minding to content you,
> Our true intent is. All for your delight,
> We are not here. That you should here repent you,
> The actors are at hand. . . .

Readers of the plays find an overabundance of apostrophes in the words, indicating that a letter has been left out, as in the familiar "ne'er" and "o'er," but also in the uncommon verb ending "'d." With "ne'er" and "o'er" he indicates that these normally two syllable words are to be said as one syllable, and on other occasions that two words are to be similarly compressed, as with "i'th" (in the) and "o'th" (of the). At times he will simply leave to our understanding that two words are to be accepted as one, as in the iambic measure of the familiar "To be, or not to be, that is the question," where the words "is the" are slurred together.

The apostrophe, then, will indicate that a syllable commonly pronounced is not to be spoken, as when Polonius says of Hamlet that he has "from his senses fall'n thereon," and Shylock complains that his ducats have been "stol'n by my daughter." The verb ending "ed" is frequently reduced to "'d," even in words where it does not constitute a syllable anyway, as in Richard III's complaint that he was born "deform'd, unfinish'd." But Shakespeare is making a distinction here between when he wants it pronounced and when he doesn't. He preserves the "ed" spelling in words where it is to be spoken even though it is not sounded in common speech. We have, for example, Juliet's lament on hearing of Romeo's sentence, "Tybalt is dead, and Romeo banishèd. / That 'banished,' that one word 'banished,' / Hath slain ten thousand Tybalts." Again, when the young lovers of *The Tempest* meet, Ferdinand is immediately smitten by his "Admired Miranda," and Portia advises Shylock that mercy "becomes / The thronèd monarch better than his crown."

Shakespeare will occasionally omit small words to maintain the meter, leaving it to us to supply them. Ferdinand praises Prospero as "so rare a wond'red father, and a wise," where it would appear he means "wise one"; and in the lament of Claudius that "When sorrows come, they come not single spies, / But in battalions," where we will silently provide an "in" or "as" before "single spies." Shakespeare will also invert the normally expected order of words to produce the poetic effect, as when Othello, gazing on the sleeping Desdemona, vows that he will not "scar that whiter skin of hers than snow." More examples could be cited, but these few will alert playgoers that poetic passages will often depart from the patterns of everyday speech. Again, all of these devices are employed to sustain the meter and the pentameter line.

In a sense, our enjoyment of the rhythm of poetry arises from the seemingly contradictory experience of knowing it's there but remaining largely unaware of it. An actor speaking the lines must take care to avoid drawing attention to the meter by too heavy an emphasis or a singsong, nursery-rhyme delivery. If the rhythm is too obvious, the effect is lost. Ideally it should be felt rather than heard, escaping conscious notice and vibrating on the natural pulses of our being.

SOUND: RHYME AND ALLITERATION

The sounds of music and poetry have a like effect. As their common rhythms resonate on the tempos of nature, so also do their notes and words on its sounds. Indeed, sound itself, scientists tell us, is but another form of rhythm, of unseen waves that rise and fall, advance and recede in the air about us. Nature has a music of its own: the song of birds, the cacophony of flying geese, a stream rushing over rocks, the rustle of leaf-heavy boughs in a summer breeze. And its sounds have the power to evoke emotions: a bolt of lightning excites fear, the lapping of lake water a sense of ease, the crash of angry waves wonder. Some produce a compound of emotions—a rumbling of the earth both fear and awe, the cry of a child in the night both pity and anxiety.

Music moves us in the same way, perhaps because it echoes these natural sounds, appealing to something deep within us, skirting the conscious mind to touch some primal core of our being. A melody, which is but a succession of sounds, can have a profound effect upon the listener. In one respect, it can call to mind some important lifetime episode—a love song popular during courtship, another that brings to mind the sad ending of a marriage or affair, or a childhood jingle recalling a time of happy innocence. But these are all personal, not universal, responses, depending for their effect upon the faculty of memory. The puzzling enigma is how music moves us in the first place, what causes the fibers of our being to vibrate in sympathy with it.

In the final analysis, music is a mystery, but something may be said of its effects. A melody, a lyric, a theme, whatever term may apply to it, may be just a sequence of sounds, but it has a curious appeal in that, once heard, it provokes a desire to be heard again. Teenagers will play a favorite recording over and over (to the distress of their parents), and opera lovers will return time and again to hear a familiar aria. And our response to these sounds can vary greatly: a solemn chant rising through cathedral arches can induce reverence, a thunderous symphony stir the blood, a tinkling nursery song delight a child, a lilting melody reduce a lover to jelly. Music can make us laugh, or weep, or rage.

Again, what notes are to music, words are to poetry. We may not fully understand *why* a repetition of sounds in poetry moves our sensibilities—it is a phenomenon perhaps better left to the philosopher or psychologist to explain. But, as with music, we can explore its effects. At least three may be suggested: It is pleasurable to the ear. It captures the attention, that is, hearing the sound of a word arouses the expectation of its recurrence. And it raises the emotional intensity of the moment. It is the last effect that comes closest to our subject here, the enjoyment of a play. The repetition of sound, then, raises the fervor of a dramatic moment to a higher level, whether the emotion be love, anger, outrage, or sorrow. And that heightened effect is achieved by two kinds of verbal repetition: rhyme and alliteration.

Before Shakespeare's time, rhyme was considered indispensable to English lyric and dramatic poetry, as much so as it is today in popular music, whether love ballads, songs of protest, modern rock, or rap. But Christopher Marlowe, Shakespeare's contemporary, introduced an innovation in his plays: unrhymed pentameter, or "blank" verse; and Shakespeare adopted "Marlowe's mighty line" as his own. His early plays are more heavily rhymed than the later great works, though he retained the tradition in the many songs scattered throughout his texts as well as in solemn ceremonial episodes and mystical incantations: "Double, double, toil and trouble. / Fire burn and cauldron bubble." It was also his practice to conclude a scene with a rhymed couplet to convey a sense of finality, or closure, to an episode, as when Hamlet descends from the battlements of Elsinore to seek the death of Claudius—"The time is out of joint. O cursed spite / That ever I was born to set it right!"—or as Macbeth counsels his wife while awaiting word of Banquo's murder—"Thou marvel'st at my words: but hold thee still; / Things had begun make strong themselves by ill."

Rhyme is highly effective in enhancing expressions of love and anger. We find both, for example, when Romeo and Juliet first meet at the Capulet's masked ball. The opening lines of the scene are all in prose and in the blank verse of Capulet's rambling reminiscence of his "dancing days." But when Romeo lays eyes on Juliet, he promptly falls in love, as do so many of Shakespeare's comic and tragic heroes. Enraptured by the sight of her, he bursts into rhyme:

> O, she doth teach the torches to burn bright.
> It seems she hangs upon the cheek of night
> As a rich jewel in an Ethiop's ear—
> Beauty too rich for use, for earth too dear. . . .
> Did my heart love till now? Foreswear it, sight!
> For I ne'er saw true beauty till this night.

But Juliet's hotheaded cousin, Tybalt, recognizing the voice of Romeo, observes the encounter between the lovers and, outraged at the insolent intrusion of a Montague into the Capulet festivities, calls for his rapier. Romeo is, in his eyes, "a villain that is hither come in spite / To scorn at our solemnity this night" and "by the stock and honor of my kin, / To strike him dead I hold it not a sin." Restrained by the elder Capulet, however, he vents his rage in ominous rhymed couplets: "I will withdraw; but his intrusion shall, / Now seeming sweet, convert to bitt'rest gall."

As the lovers come face to face, Shakespeare conveys the intensity of the meeting, not only in rhyme but in the shape of a sonnet, a verse form reserved in his time for love poetry. Romeo compares himself to a pilgrim, Juliet to a sacred shrine; and she responds coyly:

> *Romeo.*   If I profane with my unworthiest hand
>   This holy shrine, the gentle sin is this,
>   My lips, two blushing pilgrims, ready stand
>   To smooth that rough touch with a tender kiss.
> *Juliet.*   Good pilgrim, you do wrong your hand too much
>   Which mannerly devotion shows in this:
>   For saints have hands that pilgrims' hands do touch,
>   And palm to palm is holy palmer's kiss.
> *Romeo.*   Have not saints lips, and holy palmers too?
> *Juliet.*   Ay, pilgrim, lips that they must use in pray'r.
> *Romeo.*   O then, dear saint, let lips do what hands do,
>   They pray, lest faith turn to despair.
> *Juliet.*   Saints do not move, though grant for prayer's sake.
> *Romeo.*   Then move not while my prayer's effects I take.
>
>   [Kissing her.]

It is not to be expected, of course, that those in the audience seeing the play for the first time will be aware that they are hearing a sonnet, but the intensity of the moment, captured in rhyme, is unmistakable.

Rhyme can register a whole range of high emotions, as in Timon of Athens's bitter vow, "henceforth hated be / Of Timon man and all humanity." And sorrow—the grief of Titus Andronicus at the sight of his mutilated daughter, "O, what a sympathy of woe is this, / As far from help as Limbo is from bliss!" And quiet despair, as when Richard II takes final leave of his wife.

> Come, come, in wooing sorrow let's be brief,
> Since, wedding it, there is such length in grief.
> One kiss shall stop our mouths, and dumbly part;
> Thus give I mine, and thus take I thy heart. . . .
> We make woe wanton with this fond delay.
> Once more, adieu! The rest let sorrow say.

Rhymed verse, then, calls attention and lends emphasis to the passion of the moment.

As noted, Shakespeare employed rhyme more often in his early plays, but as he matured in his art he depended less upon it, preferring blank verse, which relies more on rhythm and imagery for effect. The poet had other means, however, of introducing repetitive sounds into his lines. Among them alliteration, the repetition of the same sound in successive words, as I have just done here with "s" and Richard II does with, "The rest let sorrow say."

It is difficult to pin down the precise effect of alliteration. At times the words seem to sound like what they're saying, as in Viola's quandary in *Twelfth Night*. Briefly, she enters the service of Duke Orsino in a male disguise as his young page Cesario. She falls in love with him, but the duke desires the lovely Olivia, who shuns him. So Orsino sends Viola, as Cesario, to plead for him with Olivia, and it is soon apparent that the lady has fallen in love with Viola in her male persona! It is a thorny love triangle that leaves Viola perplexed: "O time, thou must untangle this, not I, / It is too hard a knot for me t'untie." The repetition of the "n" and "t" sounds reflect Viola's dilemma, a "knotty" one indeed. Consider also Hamlet's distress at the hasty marriage of his mother: "O most wicked speed: to post / With such dexterity to incestuous sheets." The lines suggest sensuous bodies sliding across those imagined sheets. Hamlet is in anguish at the very thought of it.

As in the case of rhythm, the repetition of sounds in rhyme and alliteration is most effective when it passes unnoticed, for when it draws attention to itself it can be dismissed as deliberate artifice rather than subtle art flowing naturally from the poet's pen. Shakespeare parodies the excessively obvious use of alliteration in the prologue to *Pyramus and Thisbe* in *A Midsummer Night's Dream*, "Whereat with blade, with bloody blameful blade, / He bravely broach'd his boiling bloody breast" and in Bottom's "Quail, crush, conclude, and quell!"

On the whole, perhaps the most pervasive appeal of this repetition of sounds in poetry is that it contributes to the musical quality of the lines. Like rhythm, it is better when felt rather than heard; it cannot be so overt as to attract our notice. We are uncomfortable with a poet who mounts an obvious assault upon our senses; rather, we enjoy poetry and music the more when they move us in hidden ways.

Rhythm and rhyme call for a degree of precision when poetry is spoken in performance, and Shakespeare left us some cogent advice on this subject. Admittedly we cannot surmise what "Shakespeare thought" or "Shakespeare believed" on the evidence of his characters' speeches, but when they express an opinion on the theater we can be fairly confident that we hear the poet's authentic voice. His most incisive commentary on acting is Hamlet's advice to the players before the performance of *The Murder of Gonzago*, to which he has added, he says, "some dozen or sixteen lines":

> Speak the speech, I pray you, as I pronounced it to you, trippingly on the tongue: but if you mouth it, as many of your players do, I had as lief the town-crier spoke my lines. Nor do not saw the air too much with your hand, thus, but use all gently; for in the very torrent, tempest, and, as I may say, the whirlwind of passion, you must acquire and beget a temperance that may give it smoothness.

His counsel deserves comment. By "trippingly on the tongue" he means preserve the rhythm; avoid the actor's inclination to insert dramatic pauses to "mouth" or give undue emphasis to select words or phrases, thereby disrupting the music of the speech. It is tempting, for example, to render the famous line: "To be—or not to be—that—is the question." The ideal is "smoothness" of delivery. His advice to restrain the impulse to accompany lines with extravagant gestures—"Nor do not saw the air too much with your hand, thus, but use all gently"—is easily understood. The poet is concerned that the actor's acrobatics will draw attention from his words. Hamlet utters the age-old plea of the poet, "Don't butcher my lines!"

IMAGERY

Aside from the music of words, Shakespeare uses imagery to convey meaning and arouse emotion. Imagery differs from rhythm and sound, however, in that it appeals to memory or knowledge, to the life experience and common understanding of the hearer. There are two types essentially, simile and metaphor. Technically a simile is an image preceded by "like" or "as" ("she turned white as a sheet"); a metaphor is not. But this distinction falls short of defining the effective difference between the two: one conveys similarity, the other identity, so in a sense the metaphor may be said to have a broader scope than the simile. For example, if we want to describe a distasteful acquaintance, we might say, "He looks like a pig"; but if he is especially offensive, we would be more inclined to say, "He *is* a pig." This metaphor, then, calls up more unpleasant associations than simply appearance. Similarly, a besotted young man may say of his beloved, "She's like an angel," which again conveys an impression of her beauty. But if he says, "She *is* an angel," the description expands to include a whole range of personal qualities—her virtue, her compassion, her sweetness— all adding up to the total effect she has upon him.

Imagery plays many roles in poetry, and in prose as well, two of which stand out. First, it serves to convey the emotion of the moment. When Romeo says, "What light through yonder window breaks? It is the east / And Juliet is the sun," the image evokes the visceral adoration of the life-giving radiance of the sun. As the two prepare to part, Juliet expresses her hope and desire for the "blossoming" of their affection, "This bud of love, by summer's repining breath, / May prove a beauteous flow'r when next we meet."

Further, an image will render more familiar those sentiments that may lie outside the experience of an audience. We may never have stood before a king, but when in *Richard II* the Duke of Lancaster declares that he "may never lift / An angry arm against [God's] minister," we sense the awe that such a figure can command. We may never have felt the heat of battle, but the tension of that experience comes within the scope of our understanding when we hear Henry V urge his soldiers "unto the breach":

> Then imitate the action of a tiger:
> Stiffen the sinews, summon up the blood. . . .
> Now set the teeth, and stretch the nostril wide,
> Hold hard the breath, and bend up every spirit
> To his full height.

Shakespeare's lines are alive with imagery, its purpose to project across the footlights the emotional state of the speaker. In the inventiveness and beauty of his similes and metaphors, Shakespeare is unsurpassed. Here are just a few. Let us begin with some lines from an extended passage from *Richard II*. Old John of Gaunt describes that array of sentiments we associate with "love of country"; but he is close to death, so there is the added element of sorrow at leaving it:

> This royal throne of kings, this sceptred isle,
> This earth of majesty, this seat of Mars,
> This other Eden, demi-paradise. . . .
> This precious stone set in the silver sea. . . .
> This blessed plot, this earth, this realm, this England.

The speech is further complicated by the reason for Gaunt's outburst of devotion, his anger over the king's practice of disposing of royal lands to support his profligate court:

> This land of such dear souls, this dear dear land,
> Dear for her reputation through the world,
> Is now leas'd out—I die pronouncing it—
> Like to a tenement or pelting [paltry] farm.

The metaphors "sceptred isle," "other Eden," and "precious stone" express his love of England, and the closing simile, "Like to a tenement," both his disgust at Richard's betrayal and an old man's distress that he is powerless to do anything about it.

Shakespeare would have expected his audiences to have some knowledge of contemporary customs and events—but, alas, they pass us by. What are we to make, for example, of Kate's complaint, in *The Taming of the Shrew*, that her father insists her sister Bianca be married first: "She is your treasure, she must have a husband; / I must dance barefoot on her wedding-day, / And for your love to her lead apes to hell"? A glance at the footnotes will tell us that these are cruel sayings about old maids, who, among other things, are said to lead apes to hell rather than children to heaven. We cannot be expected to be familiar with these old saws; but we catch the drift of the lines: it is abundantly evident that Kate is angry, and jealous. To return to Hal's good-natured insults of Falstaff, at one point he refers to his fat friend as "that trunk of humors, that bolting-hutch of beastliness, that swoll'n parcel of dropsies, that huge bombard of sack, that stuff'd cloak-bag of guts, that roasted Manningtree ox with pudding in his belly." We may not know what a "bolting-hutch" is, or a "cloak-bag," or a "roasted Manningtree ox," but we are certainly aware that Hal is alluding to Falstaff's substantial girth.

Among other images that appear with some frequency in Shakespeare's lines are those that compare the stage to the world, the night to evil, the kingdom to a garden, and political strife to personal disease.

Shakespeare and his fellows in The Lord Chamberlain's Men thought of themselves as creating an entire world on their small stage. It is not insignificant that when in 1599 they built their new theater on the south bank of the Thames, they called it—*The Globe*. Perhaps the most memorable of passages to this effect is the speech of Jaques in *As You Like it*:

> All the world's a stage
> And all the men and women merely players.
> They have their exits and their entrances
> And one man in time plays many parts.

He follows with a melancholy account of the seven ages of man, the several roles that each "player" performs in a lifetime, ending in "second childishness and mere oblivion, / Sans [without] teeth, sans eyes, sans taste, sans every thing." Again, King Lear gains wisdom in his madness but gains no comfort from his demented insights: "When we are born, we cry that we are come / To this great stage of fools." Prospero compares the final curtain of a play to the ending of the world, which in its final moment "shall dissolve, / And like this insubstantial pageant faded, / Leave not a rack behind." And we recall Macbeth's grim vision of humanity: "Life's but a walking shadow, a poor player / That struts and frets his hour upon the stage / And then is heard no more." None of these images is particularly cheerful, but the analogy is apt. The playwright creates a world with his words in the small space before us, and he fills it with figures that we may come upon in any corner of the planet. Players in any age surely think of themselves in such terms.

The image of the garden as a microcosm of the world has been a favorite of poets since an ancient scribe composed the book of Genesis, and Shakespeare employs it with rich variety. We have already noted Gaunt's description of England as "This other Eden, demi-paradise." In another vein, Hamlet finds the world, and Denmark in particular, "an unweeded garden / That grows to seed. Things rank and gross in nature / Possess it merely." In *Henry V* the Duke of Burgundy pleads for peace, citing the devastation that war has brought to "this best garden of the world, / Our fertile France." In an extended metaphor from *Richard II*, Shakespeare again compares the kingdom to a garden. The Duke of York's gardener describes the fall of the king in terms of tending to the trees in his small domain. "O what a pity," he says, "that he had not so trimm'd and dress'd his land / As we this garden." He compares his duty to prune the trees under his care to the need for a king to prevent his barons from growing in pride and power. Gardeners have to "wound the bark, the skin of fruit trees" so that they do not become "over-proud in sap and blood"; and "Superfluous branches / We lop away, that bearing boughs may live" to bear fruit. It was Richard's "waste of idle hours," he concludes, that brought him down.

In times of political upheaval, Shakespeare's figures at times imagine their country beset by illness. Henry IV looks back on his reign with anguish: "O my poor kingdom, sick with civil blows!" and a citizen in *Richard III* laments "this sickly land."

King John, attempting to avoid an invasion of England, entreats Cardinal Pandulph to appeal to the French king: "Then pause not, for the present time's so sick, / That present medicine must be minister'd / Or overthrow incurable ensues." Macbeth, awaiting the attack of the English army, receives the report of his wife's illness. The news sparks a larger thought, and he asks why the doctor cannot "cast / The water of my land, find her disease, / And purge it to a sound and pristine health."

And, finally, the image of night as a time of evil and day as a time of good is a commonplace in Shakespeare's expression as well as in human experience. Macbeth, for example, awaiting news of Banquo's murder, mutters, "Come seeling night, / Scarf up the tender eye of pitiful day." Hamlet, just before he comes upon Claudius at prayer, says ominously, "'Tis now the very witching time of night, / When churchyards yawn and hell itself breaths out / Contagion to the world." It is a time, he says, for deeds that "day / Would quake to look on." Shakespeare, as noted, was fond of drawing attention to poetic excess and to actors who overact. Nowhere does he parody such exuberance to comic effect so well as, again, in the *Pyramus and Thisbe* episode in *A Midsummer Night's Dream*. Here, once more, is Bottom as Pyramus emoting on the image of night in lines of deliberate excess:

> O grim-look'd night! O night with hue so black!
> O night, which ever art when day is not!
> O night, O night! alack, alack, alack,
> I fear my Thisbe's promise is forgot!

Especially elusive are Shakespeare's images that refer to classics of the ancient world, with which we may not be familiar.

Meanings can be gleaned by referring to footnotes in edited editions, but classical references can otherwise escape the notice of even the most astute modern playgoer. Consider, for example, the opening lines of the final act of *The Merchant of Venice*. We are in Belmont, Portia's country estate, where the two lovers, Lorenzo and Jessica, have taken refuge:

> *Lorenzo.*   In such a night as this, . . .
>   Troilus methinks mounted the Trojan walls,
>   And sigh'd his soul toward the Grecian tents
>   Where Cressid lay that night.
> *Jessica.*   In such a night
>   Did Thisbe fearfully o'ertrip the dew,
>   And saw the lion's shadow ere himself,
>   And ran dismayed away.
> *Lorenzo.*   In such a night
>   Stood Dido with a willow in her hand
>   Upon the wild sea banks, and waft her love
>   To come again to Carthage.
> *Jessica.*   In such a night
>   Medea gathered the enchanted herbs
>   That did renew old Aeson.

We may not be acquainted with some of these classic love stories; but it has been said, and I think truly, that we are willing to pass over such obscure allusions so long as we can, again, catch the drift of the lines. And it is clearly evident that the two are engaged in an exchange that is quite familiar to us, comparing their own devotion to the passion of legendary lovers.

Shakespeare's poetic imagery serves other purposes, of course. Some passages are puzzling, however, in that they seem to have nothing to do with what's going on. The lines neither advance nor retard the action of the play, nor do they tell us anything about the character speaking. On such occasions Shakespeare is merely exercising his poetic art to embellish his tale with passages of telling beauty; and we enjoy them, as we do a lilting operatic aria, for that beauty alone. An instance is Mercutio's much-admired "Queen Mab" speech in the first act of *Romeo and Juliet*, which seems to have little relevance to the flow of events. Why is it there? Well, it is possible to imagine a conversation in which the actor playing Mercutio complains to the playwright that he has too few lines and is upset because he is killed off halfway through, and to keep him happy the poet agrees to write him a speech about a tiny, mischievous fairy who causes dreams. Another is Queen Gertrude's description of Ophelia's death in *Hamlet*, which begins, "There is a willow grows askant the brook, / That shows his hoar leaves in the glassy stream." The lines convey a sense of sorrow at the loss, but those who hear it are no more or no less distressed at the news.

On occasion Shakespeare was fond of inserting flower passages here and there, charming lists of various blooms, such as Perdita's account in *The Winter's Tale* of those to be found in each of the four seasons. See also Oberon's description of Titania's resting place in *A Midsummer Night's Dream*:

I know a place where the wild thyme blows,
Where oxlips and the nodding violet grows,
Quite over-canopied with luscious woodbine,
With sweet mush-roses and with eglantine.

Neither passage has much to say about the character speaking, about Perdita and her predicament or the fairy king's plan for his queen. They are, again, instances of the poet pursuing his art.

How does one distinguish between those lines that are important to advancing the plot and those that form a poetic backdrop to the action? Readers have an advantage here since they can pause or return to a passage to contemplate its importance or simply savor its imagery and rhythm. Playgoers have only one shot at it, but they have the advantage of hearing it, and an actor will modulate his delivery, slowing down or speeding up, raising his voice or lowering it, to add importance to key words and lines (while observing Hamlet's advice to actors, of course). As Othello gazes after a departing Desdemona, for example, he utters his sentiments toward her:

> Excellent wretch! Perdition catch my soul
> But I do love thee! And when I love thee not,
> Chaos is come again.

The lines convey his deep love for his wife and at the same time the vulnerability of his passionate nature. An actor will speak the lines with solemn emphasis perhaps on "perdition" and "chaos."

Further, the seasoned playgoer will be alert to Shakespeare's practice of concluding a long speech with a significant summing up. Henry V is deeply disturbed to discover that his close friend, Lord Scroop, has conspired to assassinate him, and he unburdens himself at length (some fifty lines) in condemning him. The treachery leads Henry to a melancholy conclusion:

> And thus thy fall hath left a kind of blot,
> To mark the full-fraught man and best indued

With some suspicion. I will weep for thee,
For this fall of thine, methinks, is like
Another fall of man.

The king has learned a painful lesson: never again will he be able to place absolute trust in any man. Again, in the storm scene King Lear concludes his impassioned indictment of the elements and appeal to the gods for justice with a plaintive cry: "I am more sinned against than sinning!" These final images carry the full weight of meaning and emotion in such passages. Figures like "fall of man" and "sinning" raise human events to the level of timeless significance, especially for Shakespeare's early audiences, accustomed to sitting through fiery sermons on the terrors of eternal punishment.

Shakespeare's language, then, can be difficult, since the characters in a play, for the most part, are speaking poetry. If the words are obscure, their order sometimes confusing, and the imagery unfamiliar, the complexity is more than matched by the music of the poetry, which conveys an emotional depth that words alone cannot achieve. In the rhyme, rhythm, and alliteration of his lines, Shakespeare is able to move an audience, reaching to a core of meaning inaccessible to mere reason. Shakespeare's poetry is one of the glories of the English language, but it takes some getting used to, whether we experience it in print or in performance. The rewards are great, however, once the ear becomes attuned to his art, well worth the playgoer's return time and again to the book or the stage.

2

Theme

W E MOST ENJOY a performance that excites the mind as well as the senses, one that has some substance to it, that confirms or enhances what we know of life. At the heart of a play by Shakespeare, to one degree or another, lie the timeless truths of our nature, a revelation of the ways in which we interact with our fellow humans and respond to events that unfold during any lifetime. We fall in love, we grow old. We aspire to greater wealth, prestige, and power, and we envy those so endowed. We burn with hatred, are moved to pity, and lust for revenge.

We are a maze of contradictions: shunning war but restless in peace, eager for learning but nostalgic for childhood innocence, embracing freedom but demanding civic order. We find peace in the scenic sweep of forest, lake, and meadow but thrill at the spectacle of conflict in the sports arena or on the field of battle. Torn by conflicting loyalties, we waver between love and duty, independence and commitment, adventure and security, privacy and fame. We are, in the words of Alexander Pope, "the glory, jest, and riddle of the world."

This is what we are, and we ask of a play that it tell us something of ourselves, of our virtues, faults, and absurdities as human beings. We ask, then, that it have a theme, an idea, a discovery, a fact of life, otherwise we will dismiss it as shallow entertainment, to be forgotten as soon as the curtain closes. It has been said that we enjoy a performance that "takes us out of ourselves" into a world we can only imagine. I would suggest, however, that we enjoy one even more when it "takes us into ourselves," portraying who and what we are, comic or tragic players on a real world's stage.

Some of the simpler "facts of life" we discover in early childhood: fire burns and snow is cold. As we mature, however, life becomes more complex: love burns at first but can in time grow cold. And as the world unfolds, revealing itself to us, it becomes even more puzzling: people are not what they seem, envy breeds hatred, evil leads on to greater evil, and "there is special providence in the fall of a sparrow," in Hamlet's words. We may find these themes in a tragedy, a history, or a comedy, but without this core of meaning a play will fail to please. This is not to say that a play must have a "message" blaring at us in every scene. We resent being bludgeoned with propaganda, sickened with sentiment, or showered with ideological cant. As we know too well, nothing is that easy. Life is not as simple as it is cast in nursery tales—"love conquers all," "be kind to animals," or "virtue will triumph"—or in political slogans that proclaim one candidate a servant of the people and paint another as at best a hapless incompetent or at worst a scoundrel.

No, it's not that easy, and we ask of a night at the theater more than an excitement of the senses, an emotional pep rally, or an affirmation of already strongly held beliefs. A play should move us, certainly, to tears, regret, or laughter, but it should also cast light on these senses, emotions, and beliefs in such a way as to probe the follies and virtues of the human beings who feel or embrace them. It should not pass judgment on what we should or should not be. It should tell us, again, something of who and what we are.

At times so many themes are packed into a Shakespeare play that the theatergoer becomes befuddled rather than enlightened. In *Cymbeline*, for example, ideas follow on one another so rapidly that they compete to be heard, and none is satisfactorily developed. We find there, among others, love, jealousy, revenge, ambition, deception, disguise, warfare, courage in the face of adversity, the inherent virtue of the highborn coupled with the nobility of the natural man, and the cleansing cure of penitence and reconciliation. In the play's "two hours' traffic of our stage," none of these themes is pursued in any depth.

On the other hand, a play may focus on too few ideas. *Timon of Athens*, for example, discovers that friendship is fragile when one party gives while the other is content to do no more than receive, and that wealth can be used for good or ill—and that's about it. *Pericles, Prince of Tyre* tells us that virtue will triumph over vice, but little else. Such plays are less satisfactory because they fail to explore the complexity of life as we know it.

We want more of a play, and that more is to be found in the themes that thread their way through Shakespeare's greatest works. Here are a few of the ideas that give weight to the words and meaning to the actions of his characters, as we delight in their wit or shudder at their villainy.

Theme

LOVE

In Shakespeare, love appears in many contexts, between father and daughter, mother and son, and in the bond between close relatives and friends; but the most pervasive is that between a man and a woman. So we shall dwell on that relationship, as does the poet at such length. The theme lies at the heart of virtually all his comedies, with the possible exception of *The Comedy of Errors*, where it appears only briefly. The tragedies portray the great love stories, Antony and Cleopatra, Othello and Desdemona, Romeo and Juliet; and even the histories have their amorous couples, Henry VIII and Anne Boleyn, the Earl of Suffolk and Margaret of Anjou in *Henry VI, Parts 1 and 2*, and briefly at the end of *Henry V*, the king and Katherine of France. And in *Richard III* we have an unflattering parody of the entire progress of courtship in Gloucester's outlandish wooing of Anne of Warwick.

Shakespeare's plays, then, abound in tales of love. The theme touches us closely, for we have all been in love, or when very young wondered what it would be like. What does it mean? we have asked. How are we to know when it is real or feigned, constant or transitory? These are eternal questions, to which Shakespeare offers no answers; he simply places love before us in an array of characters who portray it in all its joy, pain, and uncertainty, its trial and reward. At the outset here, it should be said that Shakespeare does not presume to explain why couples fall in love. It happens without reason—an exchange of glances "across a crowded room" or a chance encounter at a street corner, as a friend once described to me his first encounter with his

31

cherished wife of twenty years. Shakespeare wisely avoids conjecture as to how it happens, occupying his pen only with the comic, or tragic, consequences of this sudden, mysterious onslaught of emotion we call love.

In *As You Like It* we find Shakespeare's most comprehensive portrayal of love in all its complexities. In brief, four couples follow the tortuous path of courtship and are married in the end. These couples illustrate three dimensions of the theme, which can serve as a pattern for our inquiry into this familiar passion: the romantic, the courtly or chivalric, and the lecherous.

The word "romantic" brings to mind the popular formula of countless Hollywood films: "Boy meets Girl. Boy loses Girl. Boy gets Girl." Shakespeare creates inventive variations on the scheme, but one factor surfaces with some frequency: Again, the two fall in love at first sight—Romeo and Juliet, Ferdinand and Miranda in *The Tempest*, Orlando and Rosalind in *As You Like It*—though at times it is the man who falls first, as does Claudio at the sight of Hero in *Much Ado About Nothing* and Lucentio when he spies Bianca in *The Taming of the Shrew*, and the woman soon responds in kind.

But in *As You Like It* the pattern can better be described as "Girl meets Boy. Girl loses Boy. Girl gets Boy" since Rosalind is the central figure of the play and indeed may be the most captivating of all Shakespeare's comic heroines. She meets Orlando at a wrestling match and rewards him with a necklace when he emerges the victor. It is a charming scene in that he is struck dumb by her presence and cannot even open his mouth to thank her. Since words fail him, when they part she must be content with her coy remark that he has "wrestled well, and overthrown / More than your enemies." Events separate them—"Girl loses

Boy"—and they meet again in the Forest of Arden, but Rosalind is in disguise as the worldly young man Ganymede. She retains her male identity and conducts what may be called a test of Orlando's devotion, all the while suffering the pangs of love herself, at one point confessing to her friend Celia that she is "many fathoms deep" in it and is miserable when "out of the sight of Orlando." Shakespeare's ladies, it seems, are fond of devising trials for their suitors. At the close of *Love's Labor's Lost*, the women impose tasks on their amorous young men, promising that if they pass the test of their devotion, they will be permitted to return and try again in a year's time. Orlando remains constant to Rosalind, despite all of Ganymede's efforts to talk him out of it, and in the end she reveals her identity and the two are wed.

Another couple who come together in *As You Like It* are Orlando's brother Oliver and Celia. Oliver earlier has schemed to kill Orlando, but having fallen in love with Celia, he conveys his entire estate to his brother, content, he says, to live a shepherd's life with her—he is unaware that she is the daughter of a duke. His conversion is a familiar instance of a man's redemption when influenced by "the love of a good woman." We do not see their courtship, but Rosalind sums it up in lines that encapsule the entire history of romantic love:

[They] no sooner met but they look'd; no sooner look'd but they lov'd; no sooner lov'd but they sigh'd; no sooner sigh'd but they ask'd one another the reason; no sooner knew the reason but they sought the remedy: and in these degrees have they made a pair of stairs to marriage, which they will climb incontinent [immediately], or else be incontinent before marriage. They are in the very wrath of love, and they will together. Clubs cannot part them.

Romantic love can be joyous. Juliet welcomes its promise: "This bud of love, by summer's repining breath, / May prove a beauteous flow'r when next we meet." When, in *Much Ado About Nothing*, Beatrice becomes convinced that Benedick loves her, she is ecstatic: "Love on," she says, "I will requite thee, / Taming my wild heart to thy loving hand." And Othello, on being reunited with Desdemona, exclaims, "I cannot speak enough of this content, / It stops me here; it is too much of joy."

It can be painful as well, especially when the lovers are parted by events. Both Romeo and Juliet respond to the news of his exile with despair, calling the word "banished" no better than "death." When Antony leaves for Rome, Cleopatra finally accepts the separation with an anguished farewell: "O, my oblivion is a very Antony, / And I am all forgotten." When the Earl of Suffolk takes leave of Margaret of Anjou in *Henry VI, Part 2*, his is a familiar sentiment: "For where thou art, there is the world itself, / And where thou art not, desolation." On a lighter note, we recall Rosalind's lament that she cannot be "out of the sight of Orlando."

Love has its trials. Fathers intrude: In *A Midsummer Night's Dream*, an irate Egeus insists that his daughter Hermia marry Demetrius rather than her lover Lysander, prompting the latter to observe philosophically that "The course of true love never did run smooth." In *The Winter's Tale*, the king forbids his son Florizel to consort with the shepherd's daughter Perdita and threatens her with a painful death should she persist in seeing him. The lovers flee Bohemia to escape his wrath. In *The Tem-*

pest, to Miranda's distress, Prospero imposes a trial on Ferdinand, denouncing him as a spy and condemning him to menial tasks because, in the father's thought, "too light winning / Make the prize light." The young man proves constant to Prospero's satisfaction, the spell is lifted, and the couple united.

Especially trying are relationships in which one party is cold to the other. A haughty Bertram rejects Helena, a wife forced upon him in *All's Well That Ends Well*, and she pursues him from France to Italy and back again to win his love. Phebe is scornful of Silvius in *As You Like It* (of which more later), and in *Measure for Measure*, Mariana languishes for five years in "the moated grange" after rejection by an unfeeling Angelo.

Love can be tragic, as in Othello's aroused suspicion of Desdemona's infidelity; and it can shake entire nations, as in Antony's passion for Cleopatra, which costs him an empire. And it can be comic—Touchstone's pursuit of the goatherd Audrey in *As You Like It*, and Falstaff's courtship of Mistress Ford in *The Merry Wives of Windsor*.

Returning to *As You Like It*, we find instances of the second category of the three mentioned earlier, courtly or chivalric love. The code of courtly love was an elaborate set of rules governing the behavior of a medieval knight to a lady of his time. According to the tradition, consummation of his love was not the object; his devotion was "pure," and all he asked was the opportunity to "serve" her. Shakespeare's most thorough portrayal of the code is to be found in *The Two Noble Kinsmen*, a dramatization of Geoffrey Chaucer's "The Knight's Tale"; but the play omits one aspect of the convention that the poet most enjoys singling out for gentle satire—the male suitor's "love sickness." In a situation where the lady rejects the stricken lover or denies him the occasion to "serve" her, or where he is unable even to catch sight of her from time to time, then, it is said, he may fall into a melancholy, waste away, and even languish in danger of dying. The symptoms of this "love sickness" are readily apparent: he seeks solitude, avoiding his usual companions; he weeps at the sound of music, neglects his appearance, loses his appetite, sighs a lot, grows pale, and in general cuts a pathetic figure.

While the image may seem somewhat fanciful and distant from our own time, similar behavior, though perhaps not life threatening, may be observed in any young man in any age afflicted with unrequited love, a hopeless passion for an unresponsive young woman. Should she remain indifferent to, or disdainful of, his affection, the pain of her rejection will cause him to react in much the same ways as his medieval predecessor. In the tradition it was said that his only recourse was to plead with her to "pity" his suffering, though the word may imply something more physical in nature. The image is not so farfetched, then, and when we encounter such a forlorn creature, in life or on stage, his distress elicits both our sympathy and our silent amusement.

In *As You Like It*, Shakespeare satirizes the courtly love tradition in two episodes, Orlando's exchange with Rosalind in disguise as the "pretty youth" Ganymede, and Silvius's pursuit of the scornful Phebe. Ganymede undertakes to convince Orlando that he is not in love with Rosalind, first observing that he doesn't look at all like a lover. He has, she insists, none of the marks of man denied the company of his lady, among them "a lean cheek, . . . a blue eye and sunken, . . . an unquestionable [silent] spirit, . . . a beard neglected." Besides, she goes on, a solitary lover tends to neglect his appearance: "Your hose should be ungarter'd, your bonnet unbanded, your sleeve un-button'd, your shoe untied, and everything about you demon-strating a careless desolation." But, she concludes, "you are no such man" and therefore cannot be in love.

Shakespeare's most engaging portrayal of the "love disease," however, is the passion of the shepherd Silvius for the peevish Phebe, who demands that he stop bothering her. First he insists that she has wounded him with her eyes. When she takes him literally, replying that she can see no evidence of wounds, he has to explain that they are the ones that "love's keen arrows make." He pleads with her, "Sweet Phebe, pity me." A complication arises when, confronted by Ganymede/Rosalind, Phebe falls in love with him/her. She decides to write Ganymede a letter; and when she condescends to employ Silvius to deliver it, he is ec-static for the opportunity to "serve" her, unfazed by her sudden affection for another:

> So holy and so perfect is my love,
> And I in such a poverty of grace,
> That I shall think it a most plenteous crop
> To glean the broken ears after the man
> That the main harvest reaps. Loose now and then
> A scatt'red smile, and that I'll live upon.

He is far gone. When later Phebe asks him to describe to Ganymede "what 'tis to love," he responds with a recital of the courtly love qualities that make up his "So holy and so perfect" devotion:

> It is to be all made of sighs and tears. . . .
> It is to be all made of faith and service. . . .
> It is to be all made of fantasy,

All made of passion and all made of wishes,
All adoration, duty and observance,
All humbleness, all patience and impatience,
All purity, all trial, all obedience;
And so am I for Phebe.

It's all a fantasy, of course, but again not unlike the imaginings of a modern-day suitor urging an unlikely union, promising "true love" forever with never so much as a mention of carnal desire (of which more later).

In the opening scenes of *Romeo and Juliet*, the hero exhibits symptoms of the "love sickness." According to his friend Benvolio, he roams the woods at night and avoids his friends. His father has observed him weeping and sighing, and during the day he locks himself in his room pulling the shades so as to suffer in darkness. The source of all his sighs and groans is Rosaline, who has rejected him; she "hath forsworn to love," he confides in his friend, "and in that vow / Do I live dead that live to tell't now." His companions persuade him to attend the Capulet ball, where the sight of Juliet dismisses all thought of Rosaline, whom we never get to see anyway.

The lovesick swain, as mentioned, is always an object of sympathy—and no little amusement—among his friends. He comes in for some good-natured ribbing because of his distracted state, as anyone who has attended a prenuptial bachelor party can attest. Romeo's friend Mercutio is especially amused, going in search of him when he disappears after the ball, calling in amiable mockery, "Romeo! Humors! Madman! Passion! Lover!" Romeo, who remains hidden, responds silently with the lover's universal complaint: "He jests at scars that never felt a wound."

Just below the surface of these idealized expressions of devotion, however, under the thin veneer of romantic and courtly love, lies the reality of the matter—physical desire. No matter how fervently lovers vow eternal devotion and the purity of their passion, or how sincere their sentiments may be, the fact remains that they are moved by appetite. Orlando may protest that he will die if Rosalind will not have him, and Silvius may describe his devotion to Phebe as "adoration," "duty," and "purity," but it is physical desire that impels this elaborate image of courtship. Shakespeare completes his survey of love in *As You Like It* with the lecherous Touchstone's attempt to seduce the simple goatherd Audrey. He has only one thing in mind and begins with some pretty speeches of the sort that may have proven effective at court, only to find that they are unintelligible to the unsophisticated Audrey. She may be simple, but she is not stupid, holding out for marriage before submitting. Touchstone is forced to comply. He enlists the services of Sir Oliver Martext, a cleric of questionable credentials, only to be reproved by a solemn Jaques. Touchstone explains to him in confidence that he would rather not be "well married," since it will provide "a good cause for me hereafter to leave my wife." In the end the two join the other couples in the wedding ceremony, but Jaques has his doubts about the union, which he predicts will last no more than two months.

Shakespeare portrays physical desire elsewhere in his plays, always discreetly staged but unmistakable in its implications. In *Measure for Measure* a frosty Angelo finds himself stricken with a totally unfamiliar passion for the virtuous Isabella, and he proposes that she can save her brother's life by "yielding up thy body to my will." In *All's Well That Ends Well*, Bertram, a soldier far from home, lusts after a young Florentine maid Diana. To the surprise and delight of both men, the ladies agree to an assignation, but under strict conditions: it will be short, in the dark, and neither will speak. Both become victims of the "bed trick": without their knowledge, a substitution is made—Mariana, whom Angelo had rejected years before, for Isabella, and Helena, the wife Bertram has spurned, for Diana. Once the switch is revealed, Angelo is compelled to marry Mariana, and all ends well when Bertram declares that he will henceforth love Helena "dearly, ever, ever dearly." Oh? In *Troilus and Cressida*, Pandarus arranges for the bedding of the lovers; and in the end, stung by Troilus's scathing denunciation, he wonders reasonably why he should be scorned for helping them do what they want to do anyway.

Thus Shakespeare explores this familiar theme in its many dimensions, portraying its idealism, its passion, and its absurdity. We watch lovers as they rejoice, despair, and burn, recalling perhaps a similar time in our own lives, or anticipating one to come.

WAR

We glance at the soldier elsewhere (see pages 83–84), but here we consider the theme of war itself. It is striking how pervasive warfare is in Shakespeare's plays. A partial list of its appearance in the works will give some notion of just how ubiquitous it is.

- English invasions of France: *Henry V*; *Henry VI*, *Parts 1* and *2*; *King John*.
- French invasions of England: *King John*, *King Lear*, and *Richard III* (the army of Henry Tudor is made up predominantly of recruits from Brittany).

- Roman civil wars: *Julius Caesar, Antony and Cleopatra*.
- Other Roman wars: Those against the Volcians in *Coriolanus*, and against the Goths in *Titus Andronicus*.
- Armed uprisings and civil wars in England: *Richard II*; *Henry IV, Parts 1* and *2*; *Henry VI, Parts 2* and *3*.
- Wars elsewhere: Troy, in *Troilus and Cressida*; Florence, in *All's Well That Ends Well*; Scotland, in *Macbeth*; Wales, in *Cymbeline*.
- In addition, plots often turn on wars, such as those between: Venice and Turkey in *Othello*, which takes the Moor to Cyprus; Athens and Thebes in *The Two Noble Kinsmen*, in which Palamon and Arcite are taken prisoner; Don Pedro and his rebellious half-brother in *Much Ado About Nothing*, which brings him and his young soldiers to Messina.

War, then, is everywhere in Shakespeare—the question is, what does he have to say about it? As with other themes, the poet does not take sides. He expresses neither approval nor disapproval of this persistent human enterprise but explores it in all its complexity—its brutality, its absurdity, its rewards, and its glory.

War, Shakespeare shows, is brutal, often claiming innocent victims. In *Henry VI, Part 3*, we witness the death of young boys slain in retaliation for earlier killings. Lord Clifford captures and murders the youthful Rutland to avenge his father's death at the hands of the Duke of York. In response, the duke's sons take the young Lancaster Prince of Wales prisoner and slaughter him, indeed do so before his mother's eyes. In the same play Henry VI witnesses the combat between two pairs of helmeted knights, in one of which the victor discovers he has slain his father, and in the other that he has killed his son. The despondent king, watching a battle from a distant vantage point, likens it to a tide contending with the wind for mastery. "Now sways it this way," he says, and "Now sways it that way," in an endless struggle in which the opposing armies are "neither conqueror nor conquered." "O piteous spectacle!" he laments, "O bloody times! / Whiles lions war and battle for their dens, / Poor harmless lambs abide their enmity."

In another vein entirely, the common soldier Thersites in *Troilus and Cressida* is scornful of the long war between the Greeks and Trojans, who are fighting absurdly, he scoffs, over "a whore and a cuckold." Watching a battle, which he takes care to avoid, he chuckles with sardonic glee at a spectacle he finds no more than an unseemly catfight: "Now they are clapper-clawing one another."

In Shakespeare's time one of the most savage acts of warfare was the "sack" of a city, when soldiers seized the occasion for wanton murder, rape, burning, and pillage of its citizens. The commander of a besieging army would call upon the city fathers to surrender, promising to keep his soldiers in check if they did, at the same time warning that if continued resistance forced him to mount an assault, his men would be free to plunder at will. Shakespeare does not offer a scene of such devastation, but on at least two occasions he describes its effects in graphic detail. Henry V demands that the citizens of Harfleur open their gates, threatening that should they not,

> why, in a moment look to see
> The blind and bloody soldier with foul hand
> Defile the locks of your shrill-shrieking daughters,

Your fathers taken by the silver beards,
And their most reverend heads dash'd to the walls;
Your naked infants spitted upon pikes,
Whiles the mad mothers with their howls confus'd
Do break the clouds.

In another instance, Timon of Athens, who hates his country-men, offers the general Alcibiades gold to pay his soldiers, urging him to sack the city:

Let not thy sword skip one.
Pity not honor'd age for his white beard,
He is an usurer. Strike me the counterfeit matron,
It is her habit only that is honest,
Herself's a bawd. Let not the virgin's cheek
Make soft thy trenchant sword. . . . Spare not the babe,
Whose dimpled smiles from fools exhaust [induce] their
    mercy.

In a scene from *Henry V*, the Duke of Burgundy prevails upon the kings of France and England to end their war, describing in a moving speech the destruction it has wrought on the land:

Alas, [peace] hath from France too long been chased,
And all her husbandry doth lie in heaps,
Corrupting in its own fertility.
Her vine, the merry cheerer of the heart,
Unprunéd, dies: her hedges even-pleached,
Like prisoners wildly over-grown with hair,
Put forth disordered twigs: her fallow leas
The darnel, hemlock, and rank fumitory

Doth root upon; while that the coulter [plow] rusts,
That should deracinate such savagery.

And on the people:

And as our vineyards, fallows, meads, and hedges,
Defective in their natures, grow to wildness,
Even so our houses, and ourselves, and children,
Have lost, or do not learn, for want of time,
The sciences that should become our country;
But grow like savages, as soldiers will,
That nothing do but meditate on blood,
To swearing, and stern looks, diffus'd attire,
And everything that seems unnatural.

In Shakespeare, then, war is "hell," and in the eyes of some, absurd. At the same time, the poet tells us, it can call forth the finest of human qualities—courage, sacrifice, dedication, loyalty, resourcefulness, compassion, perseverance in the face of adversity, and the close bond of comrades-in-arms. An inspiring leader can rouse a drooping army by his example of valor and assurance. Coriolanus is a giant in battle both within and without the walls of Corioli, rallying the fearful Roman soldiers to confront the enemy. In *Henry VI, Part 1*, Lord Talbot is a tower of English strength and resolve, "the great Alcides [Hercules] of the field," and a pattern of the ideal knight for his courtesy, his valor, and his loyalty, fighting to his death against great odds. Henry V leads his men into the breach blown in the walls of Harfleur, and later at Agincourt he lifts their spirits with stirring words. "We few, we happy few, we band of brothers," he says, will be remembered "from this day to the ending of the world" for their courage and resolve in the approaching battle. Here is the Chorus at the opening of the play's Act Four, describing the king on the eve of Agincourt:

> O now who will behold
> The royal captain of this ruin'd band
> Walking from watch to watch, from tent to tent. . . .
> Upon his royal face there is no note
> How dread an army hath enrounded him; . . .
> But freshly looks and overbears attraint [fatigue]
> With cheerful semblance and sweet majesty;
> That every wretch, pining and pale before,
> Beholding him, plucks comfort from his looks.

The objective of foreign wars is the conquest of land, the ultimate source of wealth in the Middle Ages. Civil wars are a contest for power within a kingdom, in Shakespeare almost always a struggle for the crown. In either case, the end of war is a settled peace, when old animosities are laid to rest, wounds can heal, and the people can turn their energies to more fruitful pursuits. Idealistic expectations certainly, but so say Shakespeare's kings, and modern statesmen as well, as they rejoice in an end to hostilities and herald a new era of peace and prosperity. The hope is sincere, however often it may prove ephemeral. The King of France concludes a treaty with Henry V with the confidence that "France and England, whose shores look pale / With envy of each other's happiness, / May cease their hatred." The peace proves fragile, of course, and decades of conflict ensue, chronicled by Shakespeare in *Henry VI, Parts 1* and *2*.

Edward IV is exuberant after his final victory over the armies of Lancaster in *Henry VI, Part 3*: "Farewell sour annoy! / For here, I hope, begins our lasting joy." And indeed his reign of twelve years is relatively free of strife, much to the discontent of his brother Richard, however, who is scornful of "this weak piping time of peace." With the death of Richard III at the battle of Bosworth Field, Henry Tudor foresees an end to the destructive feud between the houses of York and Lancaster, soon to be joined by his marriage to Elizabeth of York: "Now civil wounds are stopp'd, peace lives again, / That she may long live here, God say amen!" England certainly suffered from internal discord after Henry VIII ended his country's subservience to Rome, but hostile armies did not clash on English soil for more than a century and a half following his father's victory.

Thus Shakespeare explores the theme in all its dimensions. He presents the terrors, trials, and rewards of war and portrays it as an endeavor calling forth both the worst and the best in the human spirit. While philosophers and statesmen have searched passionately over the centuries for an alternative to settling the world's discords, war has been a tragically pervasive fact in human history. As such, it excites the interest of playgoers and stirs the imagination of our poets, artists, and writers of the stage and screen, whatever their sentiments on the subject.

AMBITION

Ambition is portrayed in Shakespeare most frequently as the desire for a royal crown. Rosencrantz and Guildenstern, probing for the cause of Hamlet's melancholy, suggest that it arises from the prince's disappointment that his uncle Claudius has usurped the throne, blocking his way to the succession. Hamlet is evasive, confiding in them only that Denmark seems a prison to him. They press the matter:

> *Rosencrantz.* Why, then your ambition makes it one: 'tis too narrow for your mind.
> *Hamlet.* O God! I could be bounded in a nut-shell, and count myself a king of infinite space; were it not that I have bad dreams.
> *Guildenstern.* Which dreams, indeed, are ambition: for the very substance of the ambitious is merely the shadow of a dream.
> *Hamlet.* A dream itself is but a shadow.
> *Rosencrantz.* Truly, and I hold ambition of so airy and light a quality, that it is but a shadow's shadow.

It would appear, however, that ambition is the least of Hamlet's concerns: he wants to kill the king, not so much to gain the crown as to avenge his father's murder.

Macbeth, pondering the consequences of killing King Duncan and replacing him on the throne, concludes that ambition can be self-defeating. At times it "o'er-leaps itself / And falls on the other" side. He persists nonetheless and, having killed a king to gain the throne, he lives in the fear that others may be like-minded. His suspicions lead to a reign of senseless cruelty, alienating subjects who might otherwise have remained loyal to him. Richard, Duke of Gloucester, aspires to rule England as Richard III; and he carves his way to the throne by disposing of all those who stand in the way of his ambition: a brother, a wife, two young princes, and a series of lords who are cool to his design. Like Macbeth, once crowned he suspects all about him of treachery and imposes a tyrannical reign that leaves his subjects estranged, leading to his defeat and death.

It is not always a royal crown that attracts the eye of an ambitious man. In *Henry VIII*, Cardinal Wolsey misuses his office as the lord chancellor of England to accumulate great wealth, with which he intends to buy sufficient votes in Rome to ensure his election as pope. He imposes onerous taxes on British subjects, but again his ambition "o'er-leaps itself"; he is exposed and loses everything. Edmund, the bastard son of the Earl of Gloucester in *King Lear*, resents his lowly status and determines to secure the "lands" of his half-brother, "legitimate Edgar." He succeeds in a devious scheme to discredit his brother in the earl's eyes and later seizes the opportunity to betray his father as well. He achieves his goal, inheriting the title Earl of Gloucester, and successfully repels a French invasion to become the most powerful man in England. Justice is served, however, when Edgar confronts him with his treachery and kills him in a clash of arms.

In another respect, we do not unconditionally condemn Shakespeare's aspiring villains. He even manages to generate a degree of sympathy for a figure like Edmund, who questions why "the plague of custom" should relegate an illegitimate son to inferior social status. And he fashions in Richard III a character who is so outrageously entertaining in his villainy that we delight in his duplicity.

What mother is not ambitious for her child, and how often has she suffered disappointment? In *King John*, Lady Constance pursues her son Arthur's claim to John's crown, even to fomenting a war between France and England to achieve her ends. Her hopes die, however, when Arthur falls to his death in an attempt to escape his prison. Cymbeline's Queen aspires to see Cloten, her son by a former marriage, wedded to the king's daughter Imogen. When it is disclosed that the princess has secretly married another, she attempts to poison her so that Cloten will be the sole heir to the throne. Her plan fails, her son is killed, and she dies in despair. Volumnia, the mother of Coriolanus, foresees a brilliant future for her son, raising him to be a soldier so that he will have scars as witness to his service to Rome "when he shall stand for his place." In rearing him for greatness, however, she instills in him a contempt for the ordinary citizens who fall short of his sense of duty to the state. They are angered by his arrogance, and rather then choose him for high office, they banish him from Rome, a sentence that leads to his death.

In Shakespeare, however, ambition does not always go unrewarded. At times, by either ability or chance, his characters attain their goal without self-destructing. The "Bastard" Faulconbridge in *King John* aspires to fame in battle and is disgusted when denied the opportunity. In time, however, he emerges as the inspiring leader of the English forces resisting a French invasion. And the young prince Fortinbras finally inherits the throne of Denmark at the close of *Hamlet*, though only after the members of the royal family have managed among themselves to eliminate all eligible Danes. Henry Bolingbroke realizes his ambition by leading a revolt against Richard II, a profligate and unpopular king, and replacing him on the throne as Henry IV. Henry rules for a number of years, but at a cost; he is forced to face rebellions against the crown not unlike the one he himself raised.

Despite these occasional successes, the prominent theme in the plays seems to be that when ambition leads to an initial act of treachery, the evil of that act provokes greater evil, as in Macbeth's recognition that "I am in blood / Stepped in so far, that should I wade no more, / Returning were as tedious as go o'er."

ILLUSION

The essence of the theater is illusion. Figures parade before us who may or may not have trod the earth, confronting dilemmas that are either real or imagined. These are not kings and queens on stage, we know, but actors and actresses pretending that they are. We are asked not only to accept but to participate in the illusion, to see things that aren't there. The Chorus of *Henry V* is eloquent in his appeal: "Let us," he asks, "on your imaginary forces work."

> Suppose within the girdle of these walls
> Are now confined two monarchies. . . .
> Piece out our imperfections with your thoughts. . . .
> Think, when we talk of horses, that you see them
> Printing their proud hoofs i'th'receiving earth,
> For 'tis your thoughts that now must deck our kings,
> Carry them here and there, jumping o'er times,
> Turning the accomplishment of many years
> Into an hour-glass.

Later, standing on the bare stage of *The Globe*, bathed in midafternoon sunlight, he asks again:

> Now entertain conjecture of a time
> When creeping murmur and the poring dark

Fills the wide vessel of the universe. . . .
The country cocks do crow, the clocks do toll,
And the third hour of drowsy morning name.

We are only too willing to play our part with players who are playing theirs. We know that things are not always what they seem, that they can be a great deal more, or less, or something else entirely, than they appear to be. Nature itself has its deceptions: The flash of light on a forest floor could be a color-changing chameleon or just a trick of the sun through waving boughs. The mockingbird imitates the calls of others of its kind. The even surface of a moor hides deep pools dangerous to unwary hikers. An ominous calm precedes a savage storm. In many ways, then, illusion is an inherent part of the life of the planet.

Shakespeare's concern, however, is deception in men and women, where appearance often hides reality: An outwardly prosperous man may be bankrupt and a miserly pauper possess a hoard of wealth. An ardent lover may have his eye on the fortune of an heiress. A quiet, gentle man may be found in time to be viciously obsessive, and a seemingly virtuous woman a shameless hussy. Life itself is a voyage on a sea of uncertainty, as we ponder who or what to believe—the promises of a lover or a politician, the counsel of a broker, a physician, or a seer. And at times our own vision is clouded by a desire for wealth, or love, or fame.

And what of friends? A successful politician or celebrity may at times wonder about his loyal adherents, questioning whether they follow him simply to bask in his reflected glory and in the expectation of gain. Might they not turn on him to their advantage should the opportunity present itself? Henry V learns a painful lesson about friends when he discovers that a close companion of many years has conspired with others to assassinate him. Uncovering the plot, the king rages in disappointment:

> But, O,
> What shall I say to thee, Lord Scroop, thou cruel,
> Ingrateful, savage, and inhuman creature!
> Thou that didst bear the key of all my counsels,
> That knew'st the very bottom of my soul,
> That almost might have coin'd me into gold.

Scroop's treachery, Henry concludes, is "like / Another fall of man," for now he realizes that he can never again place such a degree of trust in a "friend."

Shakespeare is quite open about the fact that he is crafting illusion. *The Taming of the Shrew*, for example, begins with a puzzling "Induction." It is an episode in an alehouse that ends with the patrons watching a group of traveling players put on the riotous tale of Petruchio and "Katherine the curst." The play itself includes a group of figures who impersonate others:

Lucentio presents himself as Cambio, a literary scholar.

His servant Tranio becomes—Lucentio.

Hortensio comes forward as Litio, a music teacher.

A stranger from Mantua plays the part of Lucentio's father.

So we in the audience end up watching a group of players who are watching a group of players who within the play assume identities not their own. Illusion within illusion within illusion! None are what they seem. This parade of impersonation makes us wonder about Petruchio's rough-and-tumble wooing of Kate. Is he really the abusive master and imperious husband he appears to be, or is he, like the others, merely putting on an act "to tame a shrew"? The play itself, then, is an illusion, and its success depends on illusions within it. We enjoy it as we do any good impersonation—the "Saturday Night Live" comic who mimics the rich and famous, or the predatory villain who misleads his victims with a show of compassionate concern.

Shakespeare's plays dwell on the theme, enacting our dilemmas, as his characters engage in essentially two types of illusion. Some don disguises to conceal *who* they are; others resort to deception to conceal *what* they are. They undertake these disguises and deceptions for motives that may be malicious or innocent, resulting in consequences that are tragic or comic. The effect of all this dissembling is heightened audience interest: we know what's going on all the time while some or all of the characters in the play do not. This element, called "dramatic irony," is essential to the success of any work for the stage; it engages the audience in events, as we both delight in the charade and await the final unmasking. We know that Ganymede is really Rosalind in *As You Like It*, though no one else in the forest, except Celia and Touchstone, is aware of it. We know that Iago means Othello harm, that Hamlet seeks the death of Claudius, that Goneril and Regan despise their father Lear, and that Falstaff is an enormous fraud. At times the revelation comes early in the play, and the interest then is in plot and counterplot. Mistress Page and Mistress Ford are aware of Falstaff's duplicity at the outset of *The Merry Wives of Windsor*, so we delight in their designs to trick him. Claudius remains ignorant of Hamlet's murderous intent until he catches a whiff of it during the performance of *The Murder of Gonzago*, and thereafter we are riveted as we watch the two circle one another warily. Iago, on the other hand, is not unmasked until the very end, and the tension mounts as we anxiously anticipate that someone—anyone!—will discover his iniquity before tragedy strikes.

First, disguises. A number of Shakespeare's heroines assume a male identity, easily done in a time when the female roles were played by prepubescent youths anyway, who would have been quite comfortable in "doublet and hose." A brief list will help here:

Rosalind as Ganymede in *As You Like It*.

Viola as Cesario in *Twelfth Night*.

Imogen as Fidele in *Cymbeline*.

Julia as Sebastian in *The Two Gentlemen of Verona*.

Portia as Balthazar in *The Merchant of Venice*.

All but Portia assume a male disguise because they must undertake a voyage of some kind, and it was considered both improper and dangerous for a woman to travel alone. Portia, of course, appears as the learned doctor-of-laws Balthazar in order to save the merchant Antonio from Shylock's knife.

We may at times wonder why these characters maintain the disguise, why, for example, Rosalind doesn't reveal herself and fly into the arms of Orlando when they meet in the Forest of Arden. Well, as suggested earlier, for what it's worth, she embarks upon an elaborate charade to test his love for her. Imogen is wandering in the wilderness of Wales in search of her husband, and there's a war on; and if Viola reveals her identity, she would be dismissed from Orsino's service, where she wants to remain since she's in love with him. We could go on. In the final analysis, any premature revelation would end the play right there, certainly not to Shakespeare's purpose. These are all comedies (*Cymbeline* has been listed in recent times as a "Romance"), and the poet is intent upon milking these masquerades of all their comic potential.

Aside from characters who conceal their identity, some are adept at masking their intentions. Shakespeare portrays no end of dissembling villains, two of whom, Iago and Richard III, are especially deceptive, and an equal number of unscrupulous comics, chief among them Falstaff in *The Merry Wives of Windsor*. In the opening scene of *Othello*, Iago confides in Roderigo: "I hate the Moor." We are never quite sure why, except for the fact that Othello has selected Cassio rather than Iago to be his lieutenant, which may seem an inadequate motive for the carnage to come—four deaths and an injured lieutenant. But Shakespeare is no more concerned with why his characters hate one another than he is why they fall in love. Hatred is a pervasive theme in both life and fiction, so he says, let's start with it and see where it leads.

Iago conceals his intent under the façade of a devoted subordinate's sincere concern for the welfare of his general. It should not be thought that Othello is especially susceptible to deception, except perhaps in matters of the heart, where he is inexperienced and unusually vulnerable. In fact Othello is no more or less blind to Iago's dissembling that anyone else in Venice or Cyprus. The Moor values him as "honest, honest Iago," but any number of others too are convinced of his loyalty and integrity, each at one time or another expressing a conviction that he is "kind" and "honest," a man of absolute "trust." Not until the very end is anyone able to penetrate this mask of comradely concern, and by then it is too late. In the final scene we have before us the "tragic loading of this bed," the fruit of Iago's hidden iniquity.

Richard III is another matter. He is no less devious, but some members of the court are fully aware of his malice. Part of his appeal is that, even in the face of their hostility, he adopts the pose of an innocent victim of unprincipled slander, protesting piously that

> I do not know that Englishman alive
> With whom my soul is any jot at odds,
> More than the infant that is born to-night.
> I thank my God for my humility.

Others see through this pretension of amity, of course, in a way that the figures in *Othello* do not. Queen Elizabeth has no doubts about Richard's infamy, nor do any members of her family, but others are deceived. His brother Clarence and the Lord Chamberlain Hastings pay for their innocent trust with their lives, as do the young princes, who find him attentively avuncular. Richard is enormously entertaining in his iniquity as we watch his rise to the throne, step by deceptive step.

In a comic vein, Sir John Falstaff, Prince Hal's irrepressibly merry companion in the *Henry IV* plays, affects the posture of a formidable warrior, a man of his word, and a great favorite of the ladies. In displaying these qualities, however, he is careful to demonstrate his swordsmanship in the safety of an alehouse; when asked to pay his many debts, he bristles at the insult to his good name; and he promises marriage to a pining widow while bouncing a whore on his knee. He is, in brief, a giant fraud, but one so witty and infectiously entertaining that we forgive him his pretensions. Indeed, some admiring critics insist that his posturing is so outrageous as to be openly transparent, that it is a form of self-mockery, playing a part for the amusement of his friends. It has been suggested, for example, that he is actually a man of great courage, who acts the coward so that his extravagant claims to valor will draw laughter. Which is the reality, then, and which the illusion of Falstaff?

In *The Merry Wives of Windsor*, Falstaff is not so subtle, his charades much less many-layered. He is supremely confident in his appeal to the ladies, in this case two proper matrons of the community. He undertakes to seduce them because they hold the keys to their husbands' wealth, and he means to make them his "exchequers," as he puts it. They are outraged at his presumption and conspire to trick him by agreeing to assignations during which they set out to punish him for his effrontery. He will pretend to be the ardent lover and they will pretend to be captured by his charms. Listen to him greet Mistress Ford:

> Have I caught thee, my heavenly jewel? Why, now let me die, for I have liv'd long enough. This is the period of my ambition. O this blessed hour!

And to her reply: "O sweet Sir John! . . . Well, heaven knows how I love you, and you shall one day find it."

The outcome is a series of encounters in which Falstaff is hilariously humiliated. In one, to escape discovery by an irate husband, he is forced to hide in a hamper of dirty clothes and is then dumped unceremoniously into the river. In another he has to adopt the disguise of an old woman and receives a painful beating anyway. And finally he is frightened out of his wits when the residents of Windsor, disguised as satyrs, fairies, and hobgoblins, surprise him at night in the forest. In *The Merry Wives of Windsor*, then, Falstaff is detected early as the fraud he most certainly is and in the end is revealed to be. The comic complications arise from the fact that, because of his unassailable confidence in his masculine appeal, he remains blissfully unaware that others know him for what he really is.

A host of other characters hide their intent in one way or another. Hamlet is not a villain, but he does intend murder; and he attempts to deflect suspicion of his design by pretending to be temporarily deranged, by assuming an "antic disposition," as he puts it. Titus Andronicus makes use of the same device in persuading Empress Tamora to leave her two sons in his care. He kills them, bakes their remains in a pie, and serves it to her at dinner.

In another, more innocent form of deception, Shakespeare's characters don masks, some elaborate in design, others a simple cover for the eyes. The effect is the same, however; under the veil of presumed anonymity, they feel free to say and do things considered highly improper in a conventional social setting. All restraints are flouted, revelry reigns, and customary behavior is suspended. On meeting Juliet at the Capulets' masked ball, for example, Romeo asks her for a kiss. She agrees, not once but twice, a scandalous liberty for a properly raised young woman on first acquaintance. Family obligations are turned upside down. In *The Merchant of Venice*, during a time of Carnival, Lorenzo and his fellow masquers run off with Shylock's daughter Jessica disguised as a page, carrying with her a quantity of her father's jewels and ducats.

In *Much Ado About Nothing*, the artifice of masks is more complex. At Leonato's masked ball, for example, Hero, who has scarcely uttered a word to that point, sheds her maidenly modesty and flirts wittily with Don Pedro. The encounter between Beatrice and Benedick is comically deceptive. Both are masked and both, though aware of the other's identity, pretend to be ignorant of it. Beatrice knows she is speaking to Benedick, but he doesn't know that she knows him. Thus she can say things to and about him that she would otherwise be reticent to express. She continues to insult him, but now more sharply; he is, she says, "the Prince's jester, a very dull fool." And in a revealing moment she confesses her secret affection for him. When Benedick, in his anonymous guise, asks what man she means, she gazes wistfully out on the dance floor, comparing the scene to a crowded harbor: "I am sure he is in the fleet; I would he had boarded me." Benedick is so incensed at her calling him "a dull fool" that her remark fails to register on him.

Thus this theme, this idea, this truth of our nature, whatever term may apply to it, pervades the plays of Shakespeare. There are times, to be sure, when we are called upon to suspend our disbelief in a disguise or a deception: Would Rosalind's father really fail to recognize his daughter even though she's dressed in "doublet and hose"? And would Bassanio not detect his Portia under those legal robes? Well, perhaps, but there's fun to be had, so we'll agree to the charade, however unlikely it may be.

Shakespeare employs the theme with artful variety, emphasizing the importance of accepting our fellow humans for what they are, even when they stubbornly persist in presenting themselves as something they're not. His parade of deception mirrors the dilemma, or in the words of *Twelfth Night*'s bewildered Feste, "Nothing that is so is so!" Have we found that at times a close friend may betray a trust, or a loyal adherent intend harm to one he seems to admire? Well, yes, as both Henry V and Othello discover to their distress. Could an apparently ardent lover pay court to a maid for reasons other than sincere devotion? Yes again, as Falstaff and Touchstone ably illustrate. It's all part of life, and so it's an appropriate part of the stage as well.

We could explore further, examining any number of the themes that provide substance and meaning to these plays. Many others thread their way through the lines: the nature of evil, the role of the supernatural in human affairs, and the struggle for power, as well as some that come closer to home—the desire for revenge, the pain of loss, and coming of age. But this quick survey of these four—love, war, ambition, and illusion—will alert the playgoer to some of the ideas to be found in Shakespeare's plays and enhance the pleasure of watching them unfold.

3

Staging

IN PURSUING an evening's entertainment at a performance of a play by Shakespeare, on either stage or screen, a theatergoer may be surprised to find it in a strange setting, one other than the time or place expected, or that the poet intended. *Romeo and Juliet* may be set not in Verona but under a circus tent, with the lovers exchanging vows of eternal devotion while swinging to and fro in a trapeze act. *The Taming of the Shrew*, one may find, is a high school romance, and Othello a police chief or basketball star rather than a military commander. A performance may be set in a variety of time periods—*Hamlet* in a nineteenth-century kingdom or a modern corporate headquarters, or *As You Like It* in the art deco environment of the 1920s; the returning soldiers of *Much Ado About Nothing* may be veterans of the Spanish-American War and Richard III a military dictator out of the 1930s. The cast may be all male, quite in the tradition of Shakespeare's time, when women were forbidden the stage, or all female, which, though highly untraditional, can prove provocative: Sarah Bernhardt was renowned for her rendition of Hamlet, and a recent stage production of *The Tempest* transfigured Prospero into "Prospera."

Shakespeare's plays are not fragile; they are sturdy enough to survive a whole range of inventive variations. In *A Thousand Acres*, the film adaptation of Jane Smiley's splendid novel, for example, *King Lear* is set in a middle-America farm community; and Akira Kurosawa's *Ran* removes the play to a samurai-era Japan, with three sons rather than three daughters. We must, then, be ready for anything in attending a performance of Shakespeare, but in the end we will find it rewarding only if it truly mirrors life as he portrayed it, which is to say as we know of it, with its array of lovers and tyrants, parents and children, villains and innocents.

A performance may feature a starkly bare stage or one cluttered with scenery. The first can be highly effective, allowing emphasis on the poetry; and many of Shakespeare's plays come alive when performed in a sand pit, surrounded on several sides by an intimate audience, much as they were when originally seen. Care must be taken, however, for a spartan lack of scenery can be annoying when actors feel the need to fill the empty spaces with meaningless acrobatics. An elaborate setting, on the other hand, can be highly effective in conveying a sense of opulence (Cleopatra's sensuous court) or menace (the looming battlements and dark recesses of *Hamlet*'s Elsinore). Restraint is needed, however, for if laid on with too heavy a hand, scenery can distract from the human tensions at the heart of any episode.

Shakespeare's plays, then, are infinitely adaptable; they can be translated into most any time, location, or language, but their effectiveness depends ultimately on their fidelity to the poet's original vision. The novelty of a setting can soon pale, and if mere cleverness clouds that vision, a production may eventually grow tiresome. When stage machinery distracts from the bright core of meaning in a work—its revelation of the virtues, flaws, and dilemmas of humanity—we will emerge from the theater perhaps mildly amused but at the same time uneasily dissatisfied.

Shakespeare's imagined world may be small, set in a single space—*The Tempest*'s magic island, the castle and grounds of the King of Navarre in *Love's Labor's Lost*, or the Vienna of *Measure for Measure*. Then again, a play may range over vast distances, sweeping across an empire, as in *Antony and Cleopatra*, which carries us back and forth between Alexandria and Rome, then on to Naples, Greece, and Syria. Or it can follow the wandering Pericles to the ancient cities of Asia Minor, Antioch, Tyre, Tharsus, Pentapolis, Ephesus, and Mytilene. The diversity of Shakespeare's settings is impressive. He brought the four corners of the earth as he knew it onto his little world of the stage, distant lands that stirred the fancy of his audiences, many of whom never roamed more than twenty miles from their place of birth—except perhaps to see a play. Consider the range:

- Denmark, in *Hamlet*.
- Italy: Venice, in the first act of *Othello* and much of *The Merchant of Venice*; Verona, in *Romeo and Juliet* and *Two Gentlemen of Verona*, who then travel to Milan.
- France in *As You Like It* and *All's Well That Ends Well*, which takes us to Florence as well.
- Ancient Rome, in *Titus Andronicus*, *Julius Caesar*, *Antony and Cleopatra*, and *Coriolanus*.
- Ancient Greece, in *Timon of Athens*, *A Midsummer Night's Dream*, and *The Two Noble Kinsmen*.

- Illyria, a land lying on the eastern shore of the Adriatic Sea, in *Twelfth Night*.
- Egypt, in *Antony and Cleopatra*.
- Scotland, a separate kingdom before the reign of James I, in *Macbeth*.
- Asia Minor: Ephesus, in *The Comedy of Errors*; Troy, in *Troilus and Cressida*; Cyprus, in *Othello*; and in *Pericles*, as mentioned, a travelogue of ancient cities.
- Sicily and Bohemia in *The Winter's Tale*.
- Sicily again in *Much Ado About Nothing*, where it is a Spanish possession.
- Navarre, in *Love's Labor's Lost*.
- Vienna, in *Measure for Measure*.
- And a remote, nameless island, in *The Tempest*.

What is intriguing about this list is how few of the works are set in England. The history plays of necessity take us to London, York, Lancaster, and Northumberland, with frequent sallies across the Channel; but among the others we find only *King Lear*, *The Merry Wives of Windsor*, and *Cymbeline*, the last set in the time of the Roman Empire. That being said, it will not escape notice that many of Shakespeare's characters are thoroughly English.

A setting plays an essential role in establishing a sense of place, always important in Shakespeare. We discover, for example, that good things happen in the woods or in a shepherd's peaceful fields while hatred and violence reign in the city or court. In *As You Like It*, the forest offers a haven for those fleeing Duke Frederick's harsh displeasure. Arden is a place, in the words of Duke Senior, where one can find "tongues in trees, books in running brooks, / Sermons in stones, and good in every thing." Love flourishes there in the setting of a play that concludes with four marriages. Duke Frederick's court, in contrast, is a scene of conflict, where brother contends with brother. He has deposed Duke Senior by force, and Oliver and Orlando grapple in jealous rage. It is a court that delights in wrestling matches where the chief attraction is "breaking of ribs."

In *The Merchant of Venice*, Portia's Belmont is a garden where love blossoms, where the night is sweet and music fills the air—and there is no want of wealth. In contrast, Venice is a place of bustling commerce, of barter, debt, and "bonds." In the city, Bassanio squanders his inheritance and survives on loans from the generous Antonio, Jessica steals her father's ducats and jewels, and the Jew seeks vengeance for centuries of Christian oppression.

In *Antony and Cleopatra*, the difference between Alexandria and Rome plays an essential role in the fate of the lovers. Cleopatra's palace is a pleasure dome, a royal court given over to the unrestrained pursuit of sensual satisfaction, to elaborate feasts and entertainments ending in amorous trysts. In Rome, on the other hand, grave men talk solemnly of treaties and alliances, of war and governance. The place defines the characters that dwell in it; and in the end Rome's sober statesmen prevail over Alexandria's careless revelers.

When Shakespeare sat quill in hand, he had in mind a theater very different from those we are accustomed to. His plays were first staged in the Theater, north of London, and later in the Globe, on the south bank of the Thames, structures that were roughly circular in shape and open to the sky. A faithful replica of the Globe has been erected close to its original site, where audiences can experience a play as did Londoners four hundred years ago. There is some dispute about its exact dimensions—whether it was seventy-one or a hundred feet in diameter, for example, and how many sides it had—but a visitor today can see Shakespeare's "wooden O" essentially as he did. It was three stories high with tiers of covered galleries surrounding an open space. The stage itself, covered by a canopy, jutted out into that space and was backed by a "tiring house" from which actors emerged and where costumes and props were stored. A full house, it is said, could number as many as two thousand patrons, composed of the "groundlings" who paid their penny to stand clustered about the stage, and the more well-to-do who could afford a higher fee to sit on narrow benches in the covered galleries.

Performances, held under an open sky, were subject to the vagaries of London weather, and in the absence of artificial lighting they were scheduled during daylight hours. Shakespeare had to adapt his art to these conditions, and to convey the impression of the setting and rising of the sun while it shone brightly overhead. He did so in the poetry of his lines with occasional references to the time of day or night, some of them quite memorable. We have Horatio's "But look, the morn in russet mantle clad / Walks o'er the dew of yon high eastward hill"; Hamlet's "'Tis now the very witching hour of night, / When churchyards yawn and hell itself breathes out / Contagion to the world"; and Oberon's arch salutation to his queen in *A Midsummer Night's Dream*, "Well met by moonlight, proud Titania." He was even able to portray an ominously overcast day, like the one following Macbeth's murder of King Duncan:

Thou seest the heavens, as troubled with man's acts,
Threatens his bloody stage. By the clock 'tis day,
And yet dark night strangles the traveling lamp [the sun].

Why, the speaker puzzles, should murderous darkness "the face of earth entomb, / When living light should kiss it?"

Because of the timing of a performance, which was conducted ideally under a cloudless sky, Shakespeare found it necessary on occasion to describe weather conditions, and he did so again in the lines. In the opening scene of *The Tempest*, for example, we are asked to imagine a storm at sea, an effect he projected in the urgent orders and frantic scrambling of the stricken vessel's sailors. Perhaps the most vivid of such passages is Lear's famous storm scene:

Blow, winds, and crack your cheeks! Rage! Blow!
You cataracts and hurricanoes, spout
Till you have drench'd our steeples, drown'd the cocks!
. . . . And thou, all shaking thunder
Strike flat the thick rotundity o'th'world!

It is unfortunate that this scene is staged so realistically in modern screen adaptations of the play. All too often Lear rages under the assault of torrents of rain, howling wind, lightning, and thunder, with the result that his anguish is obscured in all the noise, drowned out by special effects. On the stage of the Globe, however, his lines were heard in all their glory.

Costumes were elaborate at the Globe—the young men in colorful "doublet and hose," the kings and queens in the robes of royalty, knights in armor, and battle-weary soldiers as Henry V describes them: "Our gayness and our gilt is all besmirch'd / With rainy marching in the painful field." Boys played female parts appropriately wigged, their trim figures rounded with suggestive padding. This requirement demanded restraint in the staging of love scenes at the time. Modern productions have the liberty of portraying lovers in prolonged clinches, devouring each other, but such episodes in the Elizabethan theater, if protracted, ran the danger of collapsing into parody. The earthy "groundlings" in "the Pit," who bellied up to the stage only a few feet from the actors, were well aware that those brocaded gowns hid the form of a prepubescent boy; and a single raucous remark drawing attention to the fact could ruin a scene. So Shakespeare had to convey the depth of the lovers' passion in the poetry. Here is Othello greeting Desdemona after he has survived a storm at sea:

> It gives me wonder great as my content
> To see you here before me. O my soul's joy!
> If after every tempest come such calms,
> May the winds blow till they have waken'd death!
> . . . . If it were now to die,
> 'Twere now to be most happy; for, I fear,
> My soul hath her content so absolute
> That not another comfort like to this
> Succeeds in unknown fate.

He concludes, "I cannot speak enough of this content, / It stops me here; it is too much of joy," and they share a discreet kiss. This is about all we actually see of their mutual passion; but it's enough.

Props were few on the Elizabethan stage. A gilded, high-backed chair might serve to designate a royal court, a tree or two a forest, and a single bed a lady's chamber. Battle scenes on modern film benefit from the service of a thousand extras; but at the Globe the clash of vast armies was recreated with half a dozen actors in blue uniforms marching onstage under a blue banner to confront a like number in red under a matching standard. They crossed swords briefly until one group was either killed or run off.

Shakespeare's audiences were asked to exercise their fancy to fill out such scenes, with various choric figures urging them to imagine more than they see. The Chorus of *Henry V*, for example, opens the play with an eloquent speech, which concludes with just such an appeal:

> Let us on your imaginary forces work. . . .
> For 'tis your thoughts that now must deck our kings,
> Carry them here and there, jumping o'er times,
> Turning th'accomplishment of many years
> Into an hour-glass."

Indeed, the same is asked of us today as we sit in a darkened theater waiting for the curtain to part on a scene that may be strange to us. And it can be said that we are in fact more likely to enjoy a play when we take part in the parade of humanity that passes before us, when our "imaginary forces" are called upon to "work"—far more likely, that is, than if we sit like empty vessels expecting only to be filled with facile entertainment.

Shakespeare's plays have proved remarkably resilient. They have survived four hundred years of revision, translation, and sometimes severe cutting; they prevail at the hands of casts that range from schoolchildren to seasoned professionals; and they retain their appeal even when subjected to disturbing distortions. His characters remain familiar whether we see them in period or modern dress, and his plays are compelling whether staged in their original setting or removed to times and places beyond the poet's imagining—a twentieth-century battlefield, a middle-America farm community, or a samurai castle. This versatility ensures that "generations yet unborn" will flock in time to theaters yet unbuilt to delight in his timeless pageant of life, whatever the setting.

4

Character

Shakespeare's plays, it is said, contain some eight hundred characters, among whom many are compelling, some less so, and some not at all. This last group includes the host of minor figures—servants, messengers, soldiers, and citizens, all necessary but nameless—who fill the stage when the occasion calls for them to appear. To their number we may add the wealth of dukes, earls, thanes, and knights in the plays, each a figure described by a modern poet as

> an attendant lord, that will do
> To swell a progress, start a scene or two,
> Advise the prince; no doubt an easy tool,
> Deferential, cautious, and meticulous.
> (T. S. Eliot, "The Love Song of J. Alfred Prufrock")

Another group includes supporting actors who are important to the progress of the plot but are largely "types" or "stock characters." They are more fully developed than the nameless "attendant" figures but undergo little change during the course of a play. They may be entertaining, or malicious, or ridiculous, but

71

they are what they are from beginning to end. These "types" are immediately recognizable and appeal in part because we know what to expect of them: if a clown appears in a scene, we anticipate foolery; if a soldier, action; if a child, innocence; if a king, authority. Among other types we encounter in Shakespeare are the smart-talking servant, the court fop, the worldly-wise nurse or handmaid, the braggart soldier, the dim-witted dupe, the Fool, and in some instances the seemingly motiveless villain.

Shakespeare portrays these "stock" figures, however, with artful variety. They fulfill expectations but never in the same way, and a glance at a few of them will illustrate that variety.

The nurse or handmaid is often older than her mistress, and invariably more worldly. Juliet's nurse is a delightfully garrulous old biddy who dotes on her young charge, remembering her fondly as a child, but she deserts her in her time of need, urging marriage to Paris even knowing that Juliet is already Romeo's wife. Desdemona's Emilia, an earthy woman-of-the-world, is perhaps less entertaining, but she remains loyal to her mistress and pays for it with her life. A variation on the figure is the "saucy maid," best exemplified by the resourceful Maria, who in *Twelfth Night* orchestrates the humiliation of the haughty Malvolio. Different as well is Charmian, who presumes to advise Cleopatra on how to retain Antony's affection. "In each thing give him way, cross him in nothing," she counsels, and receives the sharp rebuke, "Thou teachest like a fool, the way to lose him." Charmian is loyal to her queen in the end, embracing the asp so as to join her in death.

The clown, or Fool, entertains with song, dance, riddles, and a clever play on words. Shakespeare's clowns have much in common, but they display their talents in different ways. In *As*

You Like It, Touchstone is a court jester who is amusingly frustrated when he finds that his sophisticated wit is lost on the shepherds and goatherds he encounters in the Forest of Arden. On the other hand, *Twelfth Night*'s Feste seems at home wherever he goes, a traveling troubadour, content to ply his trade wherever he can find a paying audience. And Lear's Fool is a fount of common sense, daring to advise his master that "Thou shouldst not have been old till thou hadst been wise."

The "court fop" is a familiar character, elaborately costumed with a large hat which he whips off with a grand flourish in the performance of an exaggerated bow. Hotspur provides a vivid description of the figure in *Henry IV, Part 1*. While recovering from battle, he says, "Breathless and faint, leaning on my sword," he was approached by

> a certain lord, neat and trimly dress'd
> Fresh as a bridegroom, and his chin neatly reap'd. . . .
> He was perfumed like a milliner,
> And 'twixt his finger and his thumb he held
> A pouncet-box [snuff-box] which ever and anon
> He gave his nose and took't away again.

This "certain lord," Hotspur continues, demanded the prisoners taken in the battle, and

> he made me mad
> To see him shine so brisk and smell so sweet
> And talk so like a waiting-gentlewoman
> Of guns and drums and wounds.

The fop is characteristically slow-witted, to the delight of others who talk rings around him. Rosalind and Celia confuse

Le Beau with their banter in *As You Like It*, and Hamlet toys with Osric, telling him to put on his hat, then to take it off, and finally to put it back on again. Some are equally foppish and dense, though they may not be attached to a court. In *Othello* the devious Iago may easily dupe Roderigo, who is certainly obtuse, but he is less so than the simpleminded Abraham Slender in *The Merry Wives of Windsor* or Sir Andrew Aguecheek in *Twelfth Night*.

See also the "braggart soldier" or *miles gloriosus*, who talks a good war but has little taste for battle when the guns begin to roar. Pistol, in *Henry V*, is such a one. He is quick to draw his sword at an imagined affront but just as nimbly puts it away in the face of an unintimidated foe. In battle he urges others forward but scurries to safe shelter himself. Another is Parolles in *All's Well That Ends Well*, who is on fire to join in the Florentine wars but proves a weak reed when he is exposed by his fellow soldiers who pose as the enemy and capture and interrogate him. Terrified, he is eager to inform on his comrades-in-arms.

Villains come in many colors. Shakespeare attributes motives to some, but on the whole he portrays them as simply evil. They are wicked because, well, they are wicked; and, again, for the most part they are so from beginning to end, untroubled by remorse, disappointed only in that their plots are foiled. Don John is a villain in *Much Ado About Nothing*, but he is not nearly as viciously bloodthirsty as Aaron the Moor in *Titus Andronicus*. Don John simply schemes to disrupt the wedding between Claudio and Hero, while Aaron urges young men to commit rape and kills without conscience. Iago "hates the Moor," he says, because Othello promoted Cassio to lieutenant, ignoring his ancient's long service; but this seems an inadequate motive for his malice, which results in the death of four people. He is a villain—enough said!

We know all of them for what they are from the moment they step onstage; and this in part is the source of our enjoyment of these several "types," for we await the inevitable fate of each. The braggart soldier, we know, will be revealed as a coward; the fop will be disappointed in whatever he aspires to, in many cases marriage to a lady obviously out of his league; the clown will entertain; and the villain will be unmasked in the end.

The most compelling of Shakespeare's characters, however, are those that undergo a profound change of nature during a play, brought on either by forces beyond their control (Macbeth's meeting with the witches, for example) or by their own folly (his murder of Banquo). We see different sides of a complex figure forced to respond to evolving events. One may fall in love, another commit murder; yet another may be fired by ambition or reduced by sorrow. In each case they reveal a thread in that intricate fabric of emotions that defines the human spirit. In brief, they are like us, and we can see ourselves in them, for who of us has not felt the sting of envy and the heat of anger, has not aspired to fame, burned with desire, or mourned a loss.

In his short work *Of Poetry*, the Greek philosopher Aristotle addressed briefly the qualities of a character whose misfortune is most likely to arouse in us a sense of tragic loss. The figure suffers a traumatic change from good fortune to bad and responds with a comparable change in temperament. The most effective tragic character, Aristotle found, is a person of fame or high office, one with a great deal to lose, whose fall will therefore be all the more moving—a king, a prince, or, as in the case of Coriolanus and Othello, a renowned general. Further, the tragic hero should not be irredeemably evil or entirely good. In the one case—the death of Hitler, for example—we would consider the fall only just, and in the other—say, the murder of an innocent child—it would excite only a sense of outrage. The fall will appear tragic only if we can identify with figures whom we perceive as somewhat like ourselves, those who are essentially good but possessed of some defect in character, a fatal flaw that leads in the end to their downfall—Othello's passion, for example, Macbeth's ambition, or Lear's blindness to love. In the theater we witness the fate of figures in whom familiar human traits rise to the level of obsession, outweighing any goodness in them. In that sense their death can be harrowing. Only when we can see ourselves in them can they arouse our sympathy to the extent that their loss strikes us as truly tragic.

We might add to Aristotle's analysis that we are unlikely to look upon as tragic the death of a figure of advanced years, one who slips into the grave at the end of a full, rich life. In this regard, it is remarkable that Shakespeare is able to convey a sense of loss in the death of Lear, a man "fourscore and upward" in years. Nor are we likely to find tragic the loss of an infant; sad as its death may be, the babe leaves no history behind. The poet does on occasion portray the death of a child, though principally to emphasize the brutality of the villain. The murder of Macduff's son is testimony to just how far Macbeth has "waded" in blood. In *Henry VI, Part 3*, we see the slaying of young Rutland and the slaughter of Edward, Prince of Wales, as evidence of the savagery of the War of the Roses. In composing *Richard III*, Shakespeare may perhaps have thought better of such scenes, and we are spared the murder of the princes in the Tower.

This experience of recognizing our humanity in Shakespeare's characters is strange in one sense, for he parades before us figures who inhabit cultures foreign to our own, men and women who walked the earth four hundred, six hundred, even three thousand years before our time. They are, moreover, figures the likes of which few of us have ever met—emperors, kings, dukes, cardinals, and generals. And they engage in acts that are well outside our experience, deeds we can only imagine: they murder kings and slaughter the innocent, they foment wars and lead soldiers in battle, they rejoice in infamy and die of grief. Further, they embrace customs and beliefs entirely alien to modern sensibilities: Husbands look upon their wives as property, and the ladies acquiesce. Kings proclaim themselves God's anointed agents on earth, and their subjects applaud. Fathers insist on their right to choose their daughters' husbands, and the children meekly submit to their parents' will. Equally unfamiliar are the traditional costumes—men in "doublet and hose" and elaborate hats, women in brocaded gowns that cover them from chin to toe, so that a lover is reduced to writing "a woeful ballad / Made to his mistress' eyebrow" (Jaques, in *As You Like It*). And on top of all this, rather than converse in the patterns of everyday speech, they talk in verse!

This surface strangeness can be intimidating at first, leaving the impression that these characters are not our sort at all, causing us to wonder how so many hours at the theater watching such uncommon figures could possibly be enjoyable. In time, however, these kings, queens, and princes begin to look familiar, not much different, it turns out, from the fathers, mothers, and children of our own, or any other, time. And some of the dukes and duchesses are siblings who display the same rivalry and affection for one another as any in our experience. They become recognizable, despite their exalted status, as people we may encounter from time to time in the passage of our own days. And they change, as we all must, in the face of events.

FATHERS

Let us look at one or two of the fathers. Lear is a king, accustomed to unquestioned deference and obedience during his long reign, and as a result he has grown blind to love. He insists that his three daughters express their affection for him in a court ceremony with all the lords and ladies in attendance. Goneril and Regan comply with honeyed speeches, but Cordelia, the only one, it appears, who genuinely loves him, refuses to demean her devotion by putting it on public display. Her father, disappointed and humiliated by her refusal, disowns her in a fit of anger: "We / Have no such daughter." It is only after great suffering that he finally perceives her true affection and asks forgiveness for his folly.

Fathers from the beginning of time have disapproved of a son's youthful indiscretions. King Henry IV frowns on the behavior of Prince Hal. The father, like many of our acquaintance, finds fault with his son because he fails to come up to parental expectations. The prince has fallen into unsavory company, neglecting his royal duties, and Henry attributes his waywardness to a lack of gratitude or affection. The distraught father, as he lies on his deathbed, complains to his son that "Thy life did manifest thou lov'st me not, / And thou wilt have me die assur'd of it."

Fathers in any age have been known to look with displeasure on a daughter's choice of a bridegroom, but in Shakespeare's time they had considerably more say in the matter. It was accepted custom, especially among the highborn, for the father to select a husband for her, and he exercised the prerogative jealously, often responding in anger to any display of resistance to his will. In *A Midsummer Night's Dream*, Egeus insists that Hermia marry Demetrius, though she has declared her love for Lysander, and the father, calling on the laws of ancient Athens, threatens to have her put to death or committed to a nunnery for life if she disobeys him. Juliet's father is enraged by her refusal to accept Paris as a husband—unknown to him she is already married to Romeo—and he curses her savagely: "Hang thee, young baggage! Disobedient wretch! . . . beg, starve, die in the streets." And fathers react harshly to marriages conducted without their prior permission. Brabantio is so incensed by Desdemona's choice of Othello that he brings the matter before the Duke of Venice; and Cymbeline, on learning that his daughter Imogen has secretly married Posthumus, banishes him from the kingdom. Only the bravest of fathers in modern times would try to exert such authority over a daughter's choice of a mate. He may be no less upset, however, and show his disapproval in a variety of ways, most of them harmful to both himself and her.

MOTHERS

And what mother has not dreamed of great things for a son and labored to see him prosper? Volumnia envisions Coriolanus rising to the pinnacle of the Roman state and has brought him up as a soldier to realize her ambition. Gertrude is equally devoted to her Hamlet, but the relationship is more complex. Despite his rough treatment of her, she continues to dote on him, turning a blind eye, as might any mother, to evidence of shortcoming in her son. As King Claudius observes, she "lives almost by his looks." Cymbeline's queen represents the dark side of a mother's ambition. She aspires to see her son Cloten the sole heir to Britain's throne and schemes to poison the king's daughter Imogen, the only obstacle in his path.

In Shakespeare, mothers are often depicted in another role as well—the sorrowful survivors of their children. Margaret of Anjou, in *Henry VI, Part 3*, is forced to witness the slaughter of her son Edward and pleads with his murderers to kill her too. Queen Elizabeth mourns the death of her young princes, killed in the Tower by Richard III. And when Romeo is exiled from Verona, Lady Montague dies of grief. Again, while these figures are for the most part queens, they share with mothers the world over sentiments of pride in the success of their children and sorrow at their loss.

SONS

On the whole, it would appear that in Shakespeare sons remain loyal to their fathers even when the two are estranged. Prince Hal, as mentioned, never seems to be able to please his father, indeed has to save his life in battle in order to gain his approval. In *King Lear*, Edgar remains devoted to the Earl of Gloucester, even when his father orders his capture and death; and the Duke of York's four sons in the *Henry VI* trilogy resolutely support his claim to the throne. The young are often dismissive of an older generation's encrusted beliefs, but none of Shakespeare's sons actually displays rancor toward his father. The illegitimate Edmund in *King Lear* betrays Gloucester, but he doesn't hate him; he just wants his title and lands. Mutius challenges Titus Andronicus in defense of his sister and pays for the effrontery with his life, but he doesn't act out of malice. In Shakespeare we find sons who are distressed by their fathers, causing them to avoid or fear their sire; but the poet, it seems, could not bring his pen to fashion a son who despises his father—a stepfather, perhaps, as in *Hamlet*, but not a natural parent.

<hr>

DAUGHTERS

The same cannot always be said of daughters. In *The Merchant of Venice*, Jessica deeply resents Shylock, even to the extent of stealing his money and jewels when she runs off with Lorenzo; and Kate is angered to tears by Brabantio in *The Taming of the Shrew*. Goneril and Regan take pleasure in humiliating Lear, and Regan closes the castle gates on him with obvious relish, leaving the helpless old man to the merciless fury of the storm. Fathers and daughters are often at odds, as has been mentioned, over the choice of a husband for her. Some are docilely submissive to their fathers' wishes, as are Hero in *Much Ado About Nothing* and Ophelia in *Hamlet*. But more often than not the action revolves around a scheme to circumvent the parental design: Juliet, Desdemona, Anne Page in *The Merry Wives of Windsor*, Imogen in *Cymbeline*, and Hermia in *A Midsummer Night's Dream*.

BROTHERS

In Shakespeare, brothers do not always get on well, often because one is either illegitimate or younger than the other. In *King Lear*, Edmund aspires to the inheritance of "legitimate Edgar"; and in *King John*, the "Bastard," Faulconbridge, contests his brother's claim to their father's estate. Legitimate brothers can be equally quarrelsome: in *As You Like It*, Oliver is jealous of Orlando, reducing him to menial labor and denying him his inheritance because, as he says, his younger brother is "enchantingly lov'd" by the people and as a result he himself is "altogether mispris'd" by them. The two engage in a wrestling match when Orlando attempts to claim his rights. On the other hand, brothers can be resolutely loyal: Henry V enjoys the allegiance of the dukes of Gloucester and Bedford at the battle of Agincourt; and in *Henry VI, Part 3*, Edward is rescued by his brother Richard after a defeat at the hands of their Lancaster foes.

SISTERS

There are not many sisters in Shakespeare, and when they do appear, they tend to be contentious. In *King Lear*, Goneril and Regan are united in their jealousy of Cordelia because, as Goneril complains, their father "always lov'd our sister most." But they fall out later in competition for the love of Edmund, when Goneril poisons her sister and kills herself once her plots are discovered. In *The Taming of the Shrew*, Kate is envious of Bianca's many suitors and abuses her, both verbally and physically, in a jealous rage.

So Shakespeare presents us with an array of figures to be found in any far-flung family—fathers who frown on the irresponsible behavior of their sons and are vigilantly protective of their daughters; sons desperate for the approval of fathers, and daughters eager to taste the fruits of life; mothers anxiously ambitious for their children and sunk in grief at their loss; and siblings, some incessantly at odds, others loyally devoted. Shakespeare's characters, then, are not strange to us. They are indeed strikingly familiar, despite the fact that many of them are kings and queens, princes and princesses.

Aside from family members, we find figures who exhibit character traits to be found in any passing acquaintance or close friend. Among them is the cynic, who can see nothing admirable, or indeed redeemable, in the human race. Apemantus is one, in *Timon of Athens*, and Timon himself after his friends fail him in his hour of need. He retires to the forest to live a hermit's life, desiring only to avoid all human contact. Thersites is another, in *Troilus and Cressida*, where Shakespeare retells Homer's *Iliad* with acid wit. Thersites finds the Greek warriors comically absurd, all brawn and no brain. One, he says, wears "his wit in his belly and his guts in his head," and another "has not so much brains as ear-wax." Jaques, in *As You Like It*, is a variation on the figure, not bitter but gloomily melancholy about life in general. He sees the glass of humanity as always half empty and is most content when he can sit and "rail against our mistress the world, and all our misery."

And then there is the soldier. I suspect that most of those who make up modern audiences have no personal experience of war, but in all likelihood each has a grandfather who fought in World War II or Korea, a father or uncle who was in Vietnam, or a son, daughter, or friend who was in service during the Gulf Wars. We often find them understandably reticent to share with us their combat experiences, but we can discover in Shakespeare some insight into that life-shaping time. The poet provides a parade of warriors in his plays. His histories are all about wars, except for *Henry VIII*, where the conflict is domestic—the king's divorce and marriage to Anne Boleyn. Many of his tragic heroes are soldiers—Othello, Macbeth, Julius Caesar, Mark Antony, Coriolanus, Titus Andronicus—and even some of the comedies feature men-at-arms—*Troilus and Cressida*, *All's Well That Ends Well*, *The Two Noble Kinsmen*, and *Much Ado About Nothing*.

Some of these soldiers are courageous and inspiring: Henry V leading an assault through a breach in the walls of Harfleur and rallying his army in the face of daunting odds at Agincourt. See also the chivalric Lord Talbot of *Henry VI, Part 1*, who is resolutely loyal to his young king and succumbs valiantly to superior forces, witnessing the death of his son before dying himself. Some are cowardly: the flamboyant Pistol who shirks that same Harfleur breach, Parolles who "spills his guts," in a manner of speaking, when threatened, and Thersites who avoids combat at all costs. Others are thoughtful: the common soldier Williams, contemplating the fate of his soul on the night before Agincourt; and some are arrogant: a Coriolanus scornful of those who come short of his elevated sense of duty to Rome. Among them also are those eager for battle: Faulconbridge in *King John* and Fortinbras in *Hamlet*, who seek fame "even in the cannon's mouth." They are all there, and are well known to those who have been seared by the heat of battle. It should be mentioned here that nothing we know of Shakespeare would indicate that he ever served under arms. Some scholars suggest that he must have, citing as evidence his compelling depiction of war and warriors, but those images only compound our wonder at scenes that leave grizzled veterans nodding their heads and muttering, "Yes, that's how it was."

Most familiar of all, of course, are the lovers, for who of us has not been in love. Shakespeare's parade of men in pursuit of women, and women of men, ranges from the youthful and vulnerable Romeo and Juliet to the mature, worldly Antony and Cleopatra, and includes the pathetic, lovesick swain, a long-suffering Silvius in *As You Like It*, sighing that he will be content with little more than "a scatter'd smile" now and then from his unresponsive Phebe. We also find confirmed bachelors whose resolve is shattered by a pair of enchanting eyes, among them those determined to devote themselves to the cloistered pursuit of learning—Lucentio in *The Taming of the Shrew*, before he catches sight of Bianca; and the King of Navarre and his three companions in *Love's Labor's Lost*, until the arrival of the French princess and her maids-of-honor drives all thought of study from their heads. In *Much Ado About Nothing*, Benedick is resolved to "die a bachelor" until he is tricked into acknowledging that he is after all in love with Beatrice.

Shakespeare's array of characters is so vast, and his figures so familiar, that we wonder how he came to know so much about so many. Who has not known a husband eaten by jealousy at the supposed infidelity of his wife, as are Othello of Desdemona, Leontes of Hermione in *The Winter's Tale*, and Posthumus of Imogen in *Cymbeline*; or one who abandons his wife of many years for a younger paramour, as does Henry VIII for Anne Boleyn? Who of us has not heard of clerics as devious as Cardinal

Pandulph in *King John*, as compassionate as Friar Laurence in *Romeo and Juliet*, or as unintelligible as Sir Hugh Evans in *The Merry Wives of Windsor*? We all enjoy a clown as ridiculous in his pretension and his malaprops as Chief Constable Dogberry in *Much Ado About Nothing*, as absurd as the drunken butler Stephano in *The Tempest*, as engagingly witty as Feste in *Twelfth Night*, or as wise as Lear's Fool. A host of figures equally well known to us can be named. We find subordinates envious of those above them in class or office—Edmund who questions "the plague of custom" that relegates bastards to inferior social status, and Iago who resents Cassio's promotion to Othello's lieutenant. And there are many who waver indecisively in their resolve—Hamlet, of course, but also King John, Henry VI, and Richard II. There are as well those who rebel against a lifetime of oppression—Shylock the Jew and the English peasants who join in the revolt of Jack Cade in *Henry VI, Part 2*. We may not have come across an individual who is irredeemably evil, but here they are, just in case we do: Richard III, Iago, and Aaron the Moor.

So Shakespeare's characters may be found in the bosom of any modern family. And we can readily encounter a sour cynic or a happy clown, a scarred soldier or an envious villain within any city block or rural village, among school friends, or in the company of those we may chance to meet in the course of a day's work or play. And there are lovers everywhere.

Plot

Nᴏɴᴇ ᴏꜰ Shakespeare's plots is entirely original, except for *The Tempest*. All of the others he adapted from old, often-told tales (*Romeo and Juliet*), earlier plays (*Cymbeline*), collections of stories (*Othello*), poems (*Troilus and Cressida*, *The Two Noble Kinsmen*), and ancient chronicles (*Julius Caesar*, *Antony and Cleopatra*). There is evidence of an earlier *Hamlet*, for example, a play on which the poet is said to have based his own. Scholars would dearly love to examine it for keys to Shakespeare's inspiration, but, alas, it has never been found. He was indebted to the fourteenth-century poet John Gower for the plot to *Pericles, Prince of Tyre*, and indeed he acknowledged his debt by assigning Gower the role of Chorus in the play. Needless to say, Shakespeare transformed his sources, turning a poem into drama and a chronicle into poetry. *Troilus and Cressida*, like Homer's *Iliad*, opens with a conference of the Greeks and ends with the death of Hector, though much in between is Shakespeare's invention; Geoffrey Chaucer's "The Knight's Tale" becomes *The Two Noble Kinsmen*; and Plutarch's *Parallel Lives of Famous Greeks and Romans* translates into *Julius Caesar* and *Antony and Cleopatra*.

In Shakespeare, plot is the means whereby characters are brought into confrontations that ignite fires of emotion or excite laughter. The sequence of events has to make dramatic sense, of course, but its principal purpose is to provide occasion for the poetic expression of love, fear, anger, jealousy, mirth, and other familiar human responses to everyday life. What prevents Hamlet, it is asked, from dispatching Claudius when he is presented with the opportunity? This is a matter much discussed, but in terms of plot, were he to have done so, we would have been deprived of the heated encounter with his mother, the cat-and-mouse intrigue with the king, his final traumatic duel with Laertes, and a great deal of matchless poetry. Shakespeare's plots create electric moments in which human beings are laid bare, their virtues and follies exposed in all their complexity as they are brought into conflict, collusion, or mutual passion. Why does Iago so hate Othello? Well, he had been passed over for promotion to lieutenant in favor of Cassio—not sufficient reason, it seems, to justify the death of four people, but certainly enough to set in motion a series of tense encounters that lead to that tragic end. Why do people fall in love? They do for any number of incomprehensible reasons, of course; it happens, and the interesting part, the poet says, is not why it happens but what comes of it.

In Shakespeare, then, the plot serves as a vehicle to bring characters into situations where they interact in some way. In this sense it may be said that the events of *Henry IV, Part 1* lead inexorably to the confrontation between Prince Hal and Hotspur at the battle of Shrewsbury, and of both *Part 1* and *Part 2* to the rejection of Falstaff. Shakespeare is not above manipulating his plots by introducing unexpected and unexplained devices to achieve these encounters and tie up loose ends left dangling at the conclusion of a play. To this effect he occasionally resorts to what is called the *deus ex machina*. The phrase, "god out of the machine," refers to the practice in some early Greek plays of introducing a deity in the final scene to sort matters out. The actor entered from above, appropriately, lowered to the stage by a makeshift derrick, hence *ex machina*, and used his powers to resolve what appeared to be impossible complications of the plot.

Shakespeare does not resort to deities to resolve his plots, except perhaps in *Pericles*, where Diana appears to the prince in a vision, directing him to Ephesus where he is reunited with his wife Thaisa, whom he had thought dead. Jupiter thunders briefly in *Cymbeline*, but his appearance does not influence events; and Hymen descends at the end of *As You Like It*, though only to preside over the wedding ceremony—Rosalind has already resolved matters to everyone's satisfaction. In *Troilus and Cressida*, Shakespeare omits the Greek gods altogether, though in the epic poem the meddling deities manipulate events at every turn. In *King Lear*, all the characters call upon the "gods" at one time or another, but they seem to take no notice of human affairs, unless, as the blind Gloucester complains, they do so for their amusement, "As flies to wanton boys are we to the gods, / They kill us for their sport." In Shakespeare, human beings are fully capable of creating misery for themselves, without divine help.

Modern theater critics employ the phrase *deus ex machina*, to denigrate a plot that introduces gratuitous elements to resolve complications: a destitute heroine is unable to pay the rent and must submit to the advances of her lecherous landlord or be thrust out into the cold, but she is rescued by news of an inheritance from a hitherto unmentioned uncle and so can remain virtuous, and warm. Shakespeare occasionally resorts to the device. In *As You Like It*, for example, Duke Frederick is a thoroughly unpleasant man. Learning that his daughter Celia has joined his niece Rosalind in the Forest of Arden, and that Orlando, coincidentally, has taken refuge there as well, he orders Oliver to bring his brother Orlando back "dead or living" or suffer the consequences. Frustrated in his intent, he leads an armed force into the forest to put his brother Duke Senior "to the sword." Fortuitously, he meets not a god but "an old religious man," who converts him "Both from his enterprise and from the world," and in consequence he surrenders the dukedom to his brother. That takes care of him, and the happy couples can look forward to an untroubled future.

A plot can turn on as simple a device as a letter, either undelivered or intercepted. Romeo and Juliet die tragically because he fails to receive Friar Laurence's explanation of his plan to unite the lovers. And why? Because the bearer of his letter is unexpectedly locked up in a house infected by the plague. Confronted with the need to dispose of the wicked sisters in *King Lear*, Shakespeare does so with a few quick strokes of the pen. Goneril poisons Regan and writes to Edmund urging him to arrange for the death of her husband Albany in battle. Her scheme is disclosed when her letter comes into the hands of Edgar, and she kills herself. That wraps them up; now let's turn to the real subject of the play, the fate of Lear and Cordelia. In another context, the entire plot of *The Merry Wives of Windsor* is set in motion when Mistress Page and Mistress Ford receive identical love letters from Falstaff, compare notes, and resolve to punish him for his presumption.

None of these plot devices is wildly improbable, no god descending from heaven, that is; they are simply convenient ways of getting things under way or tidying up loose ends. And we'll not question them so long as they lead to tragic or comic confrontations between figures who, again, are not unlike ourselves in their ambition, passion, or folly.

Aristotle, as noted earlier, defined a tragedy as a play in which the principal character experiences a change from good fortune to bad, and a comedy, conversely, from bad fortune to good. This is a very broad definition indeed, but it is helpful in one respect as a guide to the direction of Shakespeare's plots. In the case of Othello, for example, at the opening of the tragedy he is a highly respected general of the Venetian armed forces; in the end he is dismissed from his post in disgrace and kills himself. In the early scenes of a comedy like *The Merchant of Venice*, on the other hand, Antonio is melancholy, Bassanio penniless, and Portia "aweary of this great world." At its close Bassanio is happily married to the wealthy Portia, and Antonio is reconciled to the match. In the same play, this comic plot is matched with a tragic decline: Shylock is initially a prosperous moneylender, but in the end he is left stripped of his dignity, his daughter, his wealth, and his Jewish faith.

A more modern definition of tragedy and comedy shifts the emphasis from the changing fortunes of characters to the audience's reaction to their predicaments. A play is said to be tragic if it arouses in us a sense of great loss, largely undeserved; and it is comic if it makes us laugh.

TRAGEDY

To induce this tragic sense of loss—invariably death—Shakespeare places before us figures much like ourselves, or as we perceive ourselves to be. In our own eyes we are by nature good, but we will admit to all-too-human traits that when carried to excess can incite us to acts that we would prefer forgotten. Tragic plots, then, portray characters who are subject to that excess. They sometimes fall under the spell of others. Othello, for example, is a man of passion who succumbs to Iago's sly innuendos about Desdemona's infidelity. His love is so great, it seems, that he cannot live with the thought of her betrayal. Mark Antony is a man of boundless appetite whose infatuation with Cleopatra causes him to neglect his imperial duties and leads him finally to self-destructive acts.

In other plays, inherent character traits alone can result in tragic outcomes. Hamlet, according to one interpretation, is a man who thinks too much, whose contemplative nature robs him "of the name of action" and distracts him from his design to avenge his father's murder. And the haughty arrogance of Coriolanus renders him an easy prey for those who mean him harm. Macbeth is launched on the path to his destruction by a different device entirely: the intrusion of otherworldly forces that animate an inherent ambition which might have remained dormant in him had not the witches sparked it into life with their prediction that he would be "king hereafter."

The patterns of Shakespeare's plots are certainly varied, but we can detect parallels in the rise and fall of his tragic figures which, if we are alert to them, can aid us in moving with ease and pleasure from one play to another.

It has been observed that many of Shakespeare's tragic plots follow a common pattern. A reader of his plays will be familiar with their five-act structure, but in performance the action is continuous, interrupted by one or two intermissions depending on the length of the production. The dramatic tension rises to a climactic scene somewhere about midplay. Before then the plot may develop along any number of possible paths, but after it the action moves on to its destined end. While not invariably the case, this pattern occurs often enough to provide the play-goer with a useful guide to the flow of events. Instances of the central location of such a scene can be found in a number of the tragedies. At the very midpoint of *Othello*, for example, in Act Three, Scene Two (3.2), Iago transforms the Moor from a devoted lover into a jealous husband calling for the death of his wife. Again, Julius Caesar is murdered in 3.1, and Mark Antony lets "slip the dogs of war" in 3.2. Romeo and Juliet are joyously married until he kills Tybalt in 3.1, a deed that results in his banishment and the eventual death of the lovers. And Lear's wrenching storm scene comes at 3.2. Hamlet prepares to kill Claudius in 3.3 but hesitates, a failure that leads to all his later troubles and his death.

At the same time a tragic figure's decline in fortune may follow a more linear path, a gradual deterioration in his stature and composure that starts early in the play and continues to its end. King Lear is a powerful monarch in the opening scenes, but he is reduced to a pitiful supplicant bartering with his daughters to decide who will house him, then to an anguished father raging at their ingratitude, later a madman unhinged by their cruelty, and later still a plaintive parent who pleads with Cordelia, "Pray you now, forget and forgive. / I am old and foolish," until he finally dies of grief at her loss. Titus Andronicus is a triumphant general at the opening of the play, but in response to a succession of humiliations, sorrows, and losses he declines into an impotent, grieving father who at one point appears to be losing his mind. Othello is a commanding figure as he arrives in Cyprus and is reunited with Desdemona, but thereafter the thought of her betrayal reduces him to the indignity of a skulking eavesdropper, to incoherent babbling, "Pish! Noses, ears and lips— Is't possible?—Confess—handkerchief!—O devil!" and finally to inner torment as he prepares to kill his wife.

Thus the road to tragedy can take a variety of turns in plays that dwell on common human qualities that when kept in balance can enrich life, but when embraced in excess can lead to desperation, despair, and death. We "enjoy" a moving tragedy, one that wrenches the spirit in moments of recognition, as we follow events that, we realize, might entrap any of us in a web of self-destruction.

COMEDY

Few things in life are more amusing than the spectacle of a young man or woman in love, the sight of which will induce a range of responses from a nostalgic smile to indulgent laughter. All of Shakespeare's comedies, with the possible exception of *The Comedy of Errors*, have at their heart a love story of one sort or another, even *The Merry Wives of Windsor*, where Falstaff pretends to a passion for two matrons of the town. *As You Like It* portrays no less than four loving couples in a plot that explores the subject in all its comic complexity. Most end in a happy union or reunion of the lovers, though there are exceptions: the ladies of *Love's Labor's Lost* find reason to mistrust the young men's fervent vows; Troilus ends up deserted by his Cressida; and Angelo's prurient ardor for Isabella in *Measure for Measure* is dampened by a trick.

The rich variety of Shakespeare's plots can be seen in his adherence to or departure from, once again, the familiar Hollywood formula, "Boy meets girl. Boy loses girl. Boy gets girl." We have watched this time-honored pattern of events unfold in countless films, TV productions, and live theater as well as in life itself; and we never tire of it. Shakespeare offers a parade of comic lovers, in each instance a unique variation on the meeting, the losing, and the getting. Some plots depict the traditional pattern in which the man pursues the woman, and she may return his love immediately or coyly play the game of courtship. Ferdinand is rapt in admiration at first sight of Miranda in *The Tempest*, and she of him. The same may be said of Romeo and Juliet, and Orlando and Rosalind in *As You Like It*. On other occasions the amorous young man must employ his wit and ingenuity in pursuit of the lady. In *The Taming of the Shrew*, Lucentio disguises himself as a man of letters and Hortensio as a music teacher to gain access to Bianca. In the same play we may suspect that Petruchio's rough wooing of Kate, both before and after their marriage, though ostensibly designed to "tame" her, could be but a clever device to capture her affection.

Perhaps the most protracted—and as it turns out unsuccessful—courtship is to be found in *Love's Labor's Lost*. The King of Navarre and his three companions vow to forgo the company of women and apply themselves to cloistered studies; but they are confronted with a state visit by the Princess of France accompanied, as it happens, by three ladies-in-waiting. All thought of a sequestered existence is promptly dismissed as the men pay court to the ladies. Each draws his intended into private conversation, writes amorous poems to her, and presents her with a love token. The men thinly disguise themselves as a band of burly Russians to entertain the ladies, and when the opportunity presents itself, profess their undying devotion. The ladies are reluctant, however, questioning whether that devotion will be as short-lived as their suitors' dedication to learning. They impose a series of tasks on them to prove their constancy, promising that if they are faithfully performed, the men may return in a year's time and try again.

In another variation on the pattern, Beatrice and Benedick in *Much Ado About Nothing* engage in a "merry war" of wits whenever they meet, an exchange of barbed insults designed by each, it seems, to keep the other at an emotional distance. Their friends devise a scheme to persuade them that they have been in love all along; and once their masks of disdain are discarded, they admit to a mutual passion.

In some plots men are portrayed as rivals for the affection of the lady. Bianca has no less than four suitors in *The Taming of the Shrew*, three of them in disguise. Lysander and Demetrius contend for the love of Hermia in *A Midsummer Night's Dream*; and later, under the spell of "a little western flower," they turn their attention with equal fervor to Helena. In *The Two Noble Kinsmen*, Shakespeare's comic parody of courtly love, he reworks a passage from Chaucer into a ludicrous scene where Palamon and Arcite prepare for mortal combat to decide who will win the hand of Emilia, though she has no idea who they are and would much prefer that they leave her alone. Valentine and Proteus, close friends from boyhood in *Two Gentlemen of Verona*, pursue the beauteous Sylvia, who loves the one and spurns the other. At the end of the play, in a magnanimous and highly questionable gesture of friendship, Valentine surrenders Sylvia to his comrade; but Proteus comes to his senses and returns to his first love, Julia.

Comic plots involve other devices that tickle the fancy, among them the mistaken identities of *The Comedy of Errors*, the dazzling wordplay of *Love's Labor's Lost*, and the malaprops of Dogberry in *Much Ado About Nothing* and Mistress Quickly in *The Merry Wives of Windsor*. A reader of the plays will miss the actors' antic gestures that set the theater on a roar—the double takes, pratfalls, and pie-in-the face surprises that never fail to delight. But at the heart of all this foolishness lies the most comic of human endeavors, the pursuit of love.

HISTORY

Shakespeare's history plays are especially challenging for play-goers, since they seem to presume an audience's familiarity with past events that are certainly not common knowledge today. In fact the poet took great liberties with history to produce com-pelling confrontations between characters that have a familiar ring to them, whether we know their history or not. Henry VI's Queen Margaret died in exile before the events of *Richard III*, but Shakespeare brings her very much to life and spitting venom to curse her enemies in London. Again, at the time of the battle of Shrewsbury in *Henry IV, Part 1*, Prince Hal was actually sixteen years of age and Hotspur a seasoned warrior twenty years his elder, but Shakespeare portrays them as two young men fighting on equal terms. The prince, in fact, was not even present at the battle. And when Richard II was deposed, Queen Isabel was eleven years old, but the plot had need of a woman who could project mature despair and defiance, so Shakespeare provided one. These are not historical errors. The chronicles were there to be read, and Shakespeare obviously read them with care. But he was in the business of writing plays, and he constructed his plots to bring characters together in dramatic situations—Margaret coming face to face with her husband's murderer Gloucester, Prince Hal and Hotspur in mortal combat, and Richard's queen demanding why he has submitted so meekly to "the bully Bolingbroke," a question that indeed troubles an audience as well.

History on the stage, then, need not conform to history in the chronicles. Shakespeare's plots, however, are on the whole faithful to what his contemporaries knew of events that took place almost two hundred years before their time; and they remain vivid portrayals of human action to this day, some six hundred years later. It would seem, however, that human beings have changed little over the centuries, and we recognize in the words and deeds of these long dead figures the same patterns of behavior to be observed today in those who burn with love, contend for power, seethe with hatred, or mourn a loss.

Still, a playgoer can be easily bewildered by the swift pace of events in these history plays. Some foreknowledge of plots can surely enhance enjoyment of a play populated by a dizzying array of kings, queens, and the dukes of this, that, or the other.

Shakespeare composed ten plays that chronicle English history. We shall set aside consideration of *King John* and *Henry VIII*, works infrequently staged anyway, and concentrate on the eight known as the First and Second Henriads, which dramatize events over a span of eighty-five years of that history. It should be mentioned that the First Henriad, *Henry VI, Parts 1, 2,* and *3,* and *Richard III,* were among Shakespeare's earliest plays, but they chronicle events that came *after* those he recorded later in the Second Henriad, *Richard II, Henry IV, Parts 1* and *2,* and *Henry V.* The plays dramatizing the later history, in brief, were written first, and he followed them by going back to an earlier time to compose four more. These latter, since they were the fruit of his more mature pen, are generally considered superior as works of the theater art.

That being said, let us ignore the sequence of composition and consider the plots in their historical sequence, beginning with *Richard II.* Before entering the play itself, however, some mention of prior events and figures will be helpful, since there are frequent allusions to them in the dialogue. Edward III was a warrior king who laid claim to the French crown and invaded the country, humiliating the defenders at the battles of Crécy and Poitiers. (A play, *Edward III,* has been recovered, and some scholars attribute certain passages in it to Shakespeare.) Edward had seven sons, two of whom appear in *Richard II,* the Dukes of Lancaster and York, and two others of whom we hear a great deal, Edward the Black Prince and the Duke of Gloucester, called "Woodstock" (we do meet his widow). The Black Prince, as the king's eldest son, was heir to the throne, but he died a year before his father, so the crown passed to his son Richard, who inherited it at the age of eleven and spent his formative years in the shadow of his formidable uncles (see the chart opposite).

Richard II itself dramatizes events during the final two years of his reign, 1399–1400. Briefly, the English nobility and people deeply resent Richard's imperious and profligate ways and join Henry Bolingbroke, son of the recently deceased Duke of Lancaster, in an uprising against him. He is deposed, imprisoned, and murdered, and Bolingbroke assumes the crown as Henry IV. The two parts of *Henry IV* stage the events of his reign. The central concern and chief appeal of these plays is, of course, the friendship between the king's son, Prince Hal, and his exuberant companion, Sir John Falstaff. But to the history: Henry finds that he must contend with a series of rebellions by the nobility in the north and west of England—the Earl of Northumberland and the Archbishop of York, in union with the Welsh under Owen Glendowe and the Scots under Douglas. All are led initially by Northumberland's warlike son, Henry Percy, known as Hotspur. The rebellions are crushed, the king dies, and Hal inherits the throne as Henry V.

The newly crowned king launches an invasion of France, renewing the claim of his great-grandfather, Edward III, to the French throne. He achieves a stunning victory at the battle of Agincourt and does indeed unite the two crowns. Thus ends the Second Henriad, and the First takes up where it leaves off. Soon after his triumph, Henry V is stricken with an illness while on campaign and dies, leaving as heir to the English throne a nine-month infant. The events of his reign are chronicled in the three parts of *Henry VI*.

In the absence of a strong figure on the throne during the king's minority, the proud English nobles grow contentious,

The Royal Family
(with dates of their reigns and deaths)

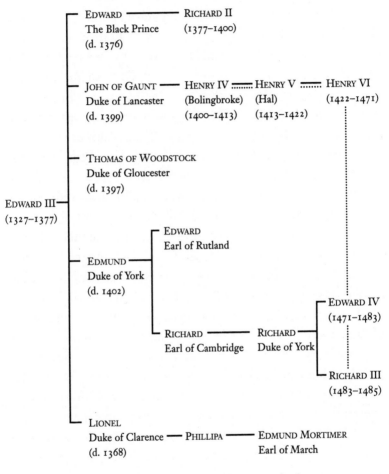

EDWARD III
(1327–1377)

EDWARD
The Black Prince
(d. 1376) ——— RICHARD II
(1377–1400)

JOHN OF GAUNT
Duke of Lancaster
(d. 1399) ——— HENRY IV
(Bolingbroke)
(1400–1413) ····· HENRY V
(Hal)
(1413–1422) ····· HENRY VI
(1422–1471)

THOMAS OF WOODSTOCK
Duke of Gloucester
(d. 1397)

EDMUND
Duke of York
(d. 1402) ——— EDWARD
Earl of Rutland

RICHARD
Earl of Cambridge ——— RICHARD
Duke of York ——— EDWARD IV
(1471–1483)

RICHARD III
(1483–1485)

LIONEL
Duke of Clarence
(d. 1368) ——— PHILLIPA ——— EDMUND MORTIMER
Earl of March

············· Line of succession to the throne

vying with one another for power and privilege. When Henry comes of age, he proves to be an ascetic, ineffectual monarch, unable or unwilling to rein in his feuding nobles, and his weakness contributes to two devastating developments. First, the English lose all that Henry V had gained in France. Second, the English nobles take opposing sides in a savage civil conflict known as the War of the Roses. Richard, Duke of York, precipitates the war by claiming that he is the legitimate king of England, arguing that since Henry's grandfather had usurped the throne illegally by deposing Richard II, his claim to the crown is corrupt. *Henry VI, Part 3* dramatizes this brutal conflict, a series of battles in which at times the forces of York are victorious, at others the armies of Lancaster, as the two houses contend for the crown. The Duke of York is killed, and his eldest son Edward inherits his claim, eventually emerging the victor in the war and mounting the throne as Edward IV. Henry VI is imprisoned and murdered in the Tower by the king's younger brother Richard, Duke of Gloucester.

This bare outline does not begin to convey the complexity of these three plays, as Shakespeare packs fifty years of violence and treachery into six or eight hours on the stage. They are, as noted, seldom produced, perhaps because the cast is prohibitively large (all those dukes and earls) and because events follow one another so swiftly, jumping back and forth between England and France, London and York, that they can easily leave an audience in a state of dissatisfied confusion. Obscured by this sweep of history, however, are some fascinating figures—Henry himself, his queen Margaret of Anjou, Joan of Arc, the valiant Lord Talbot, and the menacing Gloucester—some of whom are worthy of a play of their own.

As we know, Gloucester does indeed rate a play of his own, *Richard III*. The death of Edward IV leaves the court torn by two rival factions, on the one side the late king's family and the nobles who fought for his cause in the War of the Roses, and on the other Queen Elizabeth's relatives, a brother, two grown sons by a former marriage, and her two young ones by Edward. Richard, Duke of Gloucester, is determined to be king, and we watch this entertaining villain as he disposes of all who stand in his path to the crown. First he arranges for the murder of his brother George, and then he has the queen's older relatives executed. When he finally mounts the throne, he orders the death of her two young sons, Edward, the legitimate heir to the crown, and his brother Richard—the famous "Princes in the Tower." And along the way he eliminates anyone in the court who is cool to his designs. He meets his end at the hands of Henry Tudor, Earl of Richmond, a Lancaster by descent through an obscure line. Richmond mounts the throne as Henry VII, and to finally reconcile the two fractious houses he marries Edward IV's daughter, Elizabeth of York. This union, he proclaims, will usher in a new era of peace and prosperity for England, certainly an appropriate sentiment for Shakespeare to attribute to the founder of the Tudor line of monarchs and the grandfather of Elizabeth I.

Shakespeare's plots chronicle events of uncommon importance—the decline of empire, the rise of royal dynasties, treason, assassination, and armed rebellion. But even though the plays feature the kings and queens of history, figures from ancient myth and legend, and some gifted with supernatural powers, at the same time the course of their lives resembles in many ways the passage of our own days. They are born, come of age, fall in love, marry and beget children, march to war, strive for fame, wealth, or dominion, and they die. Shakespeare's portrayal of human experience, then, whether in tragedy, comedy, or history, is a mirror of our common humanity with its triumphs and defeats, its joys and sorrows.

Epilogue

It will pay anyone attending a play by Shakespeare to prepare for the experience, if only briefly. Those coming to a performance cold may well find themselves at times uncertain as to what is going on. The characters speak in poetry rather than the language of everyday speech and seem to be using an archaic form of English at that, sprinkled with phrases like "Zounds," "Sblood," "Prithee," "Methinks," and "By my troth." Their customs and costumes mark them as figures from another culture, and they seem to talk of matters remote from the concerns of twenty-first-century theatergoers—claims to kingship, noble lineage, insults to honor, witchcraft, ghosts, and trial by combat. As we have seen, however, many of these concerns translate readily into issues facing any culture, including our own, since those who speak of such matters are fathers, mothers, sons, and daughters engaged in the familiar pursuits of life in any age. But on first encounter the experience can be in many respects disappointing.

The difficulty lies in the strangeness of that cultural and linguistic surface. And it is critical to an enjoyment of Shakespeare that a way be found to dispel that surface so as to uncover the riches beneath. That done, we can more easily savor the moments of inspired insight, the lyric music of the poetry, and the memorable passages that have since been repeated time and again, becoming touchstones of our vision of who and what we are:

The course of true love never did run smooth.

Some are born great, some achieve greatness, and some have greatness thrust upon them.

All the world's a stage.

There is special providence in the fall of a sparrow.

I am more sinned against than sinning.

Lord, what fools these mortals be!

Some plays, it is true, need little preparation. *Romeo and Juliet*, with its "star-cross'd lovers," is familiar to any committed theatergoer, as are *Julius Caesar*, *Hamlet*, or *Macbeth*. Such well-remembered works hold hidden treasures, however, and will reward a return visit to them from time to time. But what is to be said of *Much Ado About Nothing*? Are we attuned to the verbal fireworks between Beatrice and Benedick or the malaprops of the bungling Constable Dogberry? And are we prepared for the barrage of insults that fly between Prince Hal and Falstaff in *Henry IV, Part 1* or the subtleties of Petruchio's rough wooing and mock rage in *The Taming of the Shrew*?

Of course, one way to dispel that surface strangeness is to read the play before a performance. *The Tempest*, for example, deserves to be savored slowly, for there is magic in Prospero's every line. But, realistically, busy playgoers who venture out in anticipation of an evening's entertainment after a day of labor are not likely to have the two or three hours' leisure needed for a reading. Some other way must be found to prepare for a performance; and fortunately there are any number of guides and outlines available (among them my *Theatergoer's Guide* series), works that offer at a quick glance a summary of the characters and events sufficient to provide the first-time viewer with an entry into the play. By whatever means—a book group discussion, a classroom lecture, or a conversation with an informed friend—some foreknowledge of a play will enhance the enjoyment of a performance, in the same way that, when new to opera, we found Milton Cross so helpful with his *Complete Stories of the Great Operas.*

And of course, as mentioned, these plays reward a second or third visit, as each new encounter uncovers new treasures, hitherto unnoticed. We return to see a favorite musical, *Les Miserables* or *Fiddler on the Roof,* and relish yet another production of *Carmen* or *La Boheme*; and we do so to delight anew in the music and excitement of a performance, even knowing, as we do, the fate of those who sing, fiddle, and seduce. It is the same with Shakespeare, though on first encounter the music of his lines can be at times muted by the intricate plots, the confusing parade of characters, and a poetic dialogue that can puzzle the ear. That music will emerge and those treasures surface, however, if a theatergoer is prepared by a familiarity, to any degree, with a play's plot, characters, and language. The devotion of time and attention beforehand, it will surely be found, is well spent.

Index I: By Play

Plays are cited only when reference to the works as a whole is intended. For the convenience of readers, the characters are indexed under the plays in which they appear.

Index I: By Play

Index II: Other Subjects

Index II: Other Subjects

Index II: Other Subjects